Melting the
Stone

A Journey Around My Father

Melting the
Stone

A Journey Around My Father

Richard Olivier

Spring Publications, Inc.
Woodstock, Connecticut

First American Edition
Published by Spring Publications, Inc.
299 East Quassett Road, Woodstock, CT 06281
(860) 974-3428. Printed in Canada

Distributed in the United by Continuum Publishing Group; in Canada
by McClelland and Stewart; in the United Kingdom, Eire, and Europe by
Airlift Book Co.; in Europe by Daimon Verlag; and in Austrailia by Astam
Books Pty Ltd.

Cover photo used with permission of the author. Cover and text designed by Brian O'Kelley.

Library of Congress Cataloging-in-Publication Data

Olivier, Richard, 1962-
Melting the stone : a journey around my father / Richard Olivier.
    p. cm.
Simultaneously published in London under title: Shadow of the stone
heart.
Includes bibliographical references.
ISBN 0-88214-370-0 (alk. paper)
    1. Olivier, Richard, 1962- . 2. Theatricalproducers and directors—
Great Britain—Biography. 3. Olivier, Laurence, 1907-1989-family. I. Title.
PN2598.O56A3 1996
792'.0233'092—dc20
    [B]   96-6903
                                                           CIP

Contents

Acknowledgments

My heartfelt thanks are due to the following persons: My wife and best friend, Shelley, who saw something in me that I couldn't, and never ceased her hopeful encouragement that I would one day see it for myself; my friend Jackie Leven, who knows how to throw a pebble into still waters which reaches the depths without disturbing the surface; Robert Bly, who inspired my first glimpse of mature masculinity, and generously blessed this effort by allowing me to plunder his work; Ruth Bly, who revealed the effort and solitude needed to keep a marriage alive; James Hillman, whose ability to turn an established idea on its head continues to open doors of wonder and perception; Michael Meade, whose courage to stand—alone if necessary—against the dumb giants of modern culture, is a living example of the true and vital warrior essential to create meaningful change; David Kay, who tirelessly held up a caring human mirror in which I saw my past, and held my hand while I struggled to look out of a window to the future; Wild Dance Men's Group, whose trust, honesty and support grew to contain both our selfish needs and our selfless desires; Malidoma Somé, whose blended knowledge of Western education and indigenous ritual initiation shines a unique light through the shadowy mists of the so-called civilized world; Noel Cobb, Eva Loewe, and The London Convivium for Archetypal Studies for continued support and inspiration; Roland

Phillipps and Maggie Hanbury, who helped convince me that I could write this book; Georgina Morley, Claire Evans, Ann Cooke and the staff at Macmillan, London, who nurtured its rocky path from conception to completion; Jason Wright, Chris Malcomson, Peter Hiley, Jeryl and Steve Oristaglio, and others whose reading and comments helped protect me from excess; my mother, Joan, and my sisters Tamsin and Julie-Kate, who generously understood why it had to be written; my father, whose ghost has not come back to haunt me— yet; my children, Troy and Ali, and my step-daughter Kaya, whose courage in facing the future is, quite simply, breathtaking.

The author and publishers wish to thank the following who have kindly given permission for use of copyright materials:

Jeremiah Abrams and Connie Zweig: extract from the introduction of *Meeting the Shadow,* copyright © 1991 Jeremiah Abrams and Connie Zweig. Reprinted by permission of the Putnam Publishing Group/Jeremy P. Tarcher, Inc.

Wendell Berry: "To Know the Dark," from *Farming: A Hand Book.* Copyright © 1967 Wendell Berry. Reprinted by permission of Harcourt, Brace and Company.

Bruno Bettelheim: extract from *The Uses of Enchantment -The Meaning and Importance of Fairy Tales.* Copyright © Bruno Bettelheim. Permission by Thames and Hudson Ltd.

Robert Bly: extracts from *Iron John—A Book About Men,* copyright © 1990 Robert Bly. Published by Element Books Ltd., reprinted by kind permission of Robert Bly.

"Sometimes a Man Stands Up During Dinner," extracts from "The Man Watching," "I Am Too Alone," from *Selected Poems of Rainer Maria Rilke,* edited and translated by Robert Bly, copyright © 1981 Robert Bly. Reprinted by permission of HarperCollins Publishers, Inc.

"My Father's Neck" from *Meditations on the Insatiable Soul* by Robert Bly, copyright © 1994 Robert Bly. Reprinted by permission of HarperCollins Publishers, Inc.

"I Am Not I" from *Selected Poems of Lorca and Jimenez.* Chosen and translated by Robert Bly. Copyright © 1973 Robert Bly. Published by Beacon Press. Reprinted by permission of Robert Bly.

"A Man Writes to a Part of Himself" from *The Road to Poverty and Death.* Copyright © Robert Bly. Reprinted by permission of Robert Bly. Extract from

"Listening to the Köln Concert" from *Loving a Woman in Two Worlds,* by Robert Bly, copyright © 1985 Robert Bly. Reprinted by permission of Doubleday, a division of Bantam Doubleday Dell Publishing Group Inc.

Joseph Campbell: extracts from *The Hero with a Thousand Faces.* Reprinted by permission of Paladin, an imprint of HarperCollins Publishers Ltd.

Tom Chetwynd: extract from *A Dictionary of Symbols,* copyright © 1982 Tom Chetwynd, permission of HarperCollins, London.

Shelagh Delaney: extract from *A Taste of Honey*, copyright © 1959 Theatre Workshop. Reprinted with permission.

Mircea Eliade: extract from *Rites and Symbols of Initiation—The Mysteries of Birth and Rebirth*, copyright © 1958 Mircea Eliade. Reprinted by permission of Spring Publications, Inc.

Don and Jeanne Elium: extract from "Raising A Son," copyright © 1992 Don and Jeanne Elium, by permission of Beyond Words Publishing Inc, Hillsboro, OR.

J. G. Frazer: extract from *The Golden Bough* by J. G. Frazer, reprinted by permission of Pan Macmillan.

John Guare: extract from *Six Degrees of Separation*, reprinted with the permission of Methuen London.

James Hillman: extract from *We've Had A Hundred Years of Psychotherapy—And The World's Getting Worse*, copyright © 1992 James Hillman and Michael Ventura. Reprinted with permission of James Hillman.

Extracts from lecture/workshops based on material from *Notes on White Supremacy;* copyright © 1986 Woodstock, CT, Spring Publications, by permission of James Hillman.

Rudolf Hoss: extract from *The Autobiography of Rudolf Hoss—Commandant of Auschwitz* translated by Constantine Fitz-Gibbon, New York 1959.

Sam Keen: extract from *Fire in the Belly—On Being A Man*, copyright © 1991, reprinted by permission of Bantam Books, a division of Bantam, Doubleday, Dell Publishing Group, Inc.

D. H. Lawrence: "Intimates," reprinted with the permission of Lawrence Pollinger Ltd and the Estate of Frieda Lawrence

Ravagli. Li-Young Lee: "A Story," copyright © 1990 Li-Young Lee. Reprinted from *City In Which I Love You*, with the permission of BOA Editions Ltd, 92 Park Ave, Brockport, NY.

Haki Madhubuti: "White on Black Crime," from *Earthquakes and Sunrise Missions*, copyright © Haki Madhubuti, reprinted by permission of Haki Madhubuti and Third World Press, P.O. Box 19730, Chicago, IL.

Extracts from lecture/workshop based on material to be found in *Black Men: Obsolete, Single, Dangerous—The Afrikan American Family in Transition*, copyright © 1990 Haki Madhubuti, Third World Press.

The Very Reverend Michael Mayne: *The Bidding*, written for the memorial service of Laurence Olivier, is reprinted by the kind permission of the Very Reverend Michael Mayne, Dean of Westminster.

Michael Meade: extracts from lecture/workshops based on material to be found in *Men and the Water of Life—Initiation and the Tempering of Men*, copyright © 1993 Michael Meade, HarperCollins, New York, by permission of Michael Meade.

Alice Miller: extracts from *The Drama of Being A Child* and *For Your Own Good*, reprinted with the permission of Faber and Faber Ltd.

Robert Moore and Douglas Gillette: extract from *King Warrior Magician Lover — Rediscovering the Archetypes of the Mature Masculine*, copyright © 1990 Robert Moore and Douglas Gillette, reprinted by permission of HarperCollins Publishers, Inc.

9

MELTING THE STONE

Introduction

When the heart knows sorrow
and grieves not,
it turns to stone.
> (Michael Meade, *Men and the Water of Life*)

The day that my father died my life changed. Imperceptibly at first, I began to cut off from family, friends and the world around me. Then, as the momentum grew, I threw myself into work, believing—like my father—that I would find salvation there. But it led only to greater distance and isolation.

A few months later I attended a lecture/workshop for men, run by Robert Bly, the American poet and a leading voice of the emerging American men's movement. At one point he said, "In modern society a boy cannot become a man until the day his father dies. . . ." And I knew then what I had been running away from. My task was clear, to grow up and become a man. The trouble was I did not know what that meant, or how to achieve it. Or if I wanted to.

This book is the story of the struggle that ensued, sometimes an inner battle, sometimes an outer one. I had to face the legacy of my own childhood before I could come to terms with my father. There I found a heart that had been turned to stone, and that vigorously resisted early attempts to restore feeling. When the cracks began to appear, and broke up the smooth cold exterior, there was no easy victory. Instead of the release I had imagined, I found anger and a reflex impulse to blame others for my predicament. It took a further dark journey into the shadow cast by the stone heart finally to see what I had been avoiding, and why.

Many men find it hard to move away from their fathers. My experience was exaggerated by being the son of Laurence Olivier, one of those rare men generally regarded as "the best in the world" at what he did. The easy way out would have been simply to reject him, which, at times, I tried to do. The harder task, which I eventually acknowledged to be the right one for me, was to accept him as a human being who had lived his life as well as he could.

In some ways this book is a "voyage around my father," in others a search for mature masculinity, encompassing emotion as well as thought and deed. And at times these overlap, for the father is the son's first indelible image of manhood. This search took me into close contact with the foremost figures of what is now called mytho-poetic men's work: poet Robert Bly, the mythologist Michael Meade, and archetypal psychologist James Hillman, among others. This in turn was the inspiration to set up a small men's group, and to enter analysis. Both provided invaluable frameworks within which to understand and experience what it is to be a man living at the end of the twentieth century.

Mytho-poetic work is based on images, fairy stories, poetry and ritual activities. It is unscientific, which is what makes it a valuable tool for men. We tend to pin things down, define them and put them into a neatly labeled box. But the images that arise in this work cannot be photographed; the uncovered emotional states can never be proved in a court of law.

Similarly, the implications drawn from the many memories, dreams, and flights of imagination that fill this book are personal. They are not, and could never be, facts. However extraordinary some of these may seem on the printed page, they arrived charged with emotional relevance and hidden meaning. Imagination played a vital part in this process of discovery. At times it was the only yardstick by which progress could be measured; the shift of imagery often the sole perceptible change in an apparently unchanging situation. The memories, too, are intensely subjective. Childhood experience is dredged through the mists of time by the adult brain, but felt with the intensity of the child's heart. It is only one version of the event itself, not THE TRUTH. Whatever that may be.

The story is personal, but if the events described did not also reflect the experience of others, it would not have been worth writing. I did not write this to give yet another insight into a great actor's life. I wrote this as a son trying to come to terms with his past in order to live more fully in the present, and look more clearly into the future.

I believe that we are approaching a turning point in the evolution of gender. The confusion men face today is not as obvious as the political problems around the world, nor as desperate as the social ills—though it may underlie these. The dilemma seems to be caused, at least in part, by a loss of masculine identity—and the unanswered question: "What is twenty-first century man to be?"

We are caught between male myths. The abusive and domineering Patriarch may be in his death throes, but the Sensitive New Age Guy (SNAG, appropriately enough) will not replace him for long. What form this as yet unknown man of the future takes must be looked for, debated, imagined, nurtured and brought to maturity.

One of the fundamental impulses behind men's work is to assist in this process—as the cliche has it, "to be part of the solution, not part of the problem." It is no longer enough to stay safely behind our infamous stiff upper lip and see what happens; or worse, wait for politicians, social workers, or women to fix it.

For over a generation now, women have had the courage to look at their position and redefine their collective identity. Their work has caused a shift in the traditional gender balance, which necessitates a new balance be found and a new gender deal be struck. But before such negotiations can have any real meaning we need to see what men can contribute. It is our turn for a period of honest self-examination.

One of the losses we suffer today is the lack of what our ancestors knew as rites of initiation. These ritual processes helped change boys into men, and allowed men to periodically reassess themselves and their place in society. But the form these rites took came from ancient cultures. It would not be desirable or possible to recreate them today. However, if we can recognize the need that these rites seemed to meet, and discover how they came into being, we may be able slowly to evolve a modern equivalent.

In older tribal cultures—some of which still practice initiation —an uninitiated male was known to be dangerous; to other men, to women and to himself. Recent statistics suggest that we shouldn't discount such ancient knowledge:

86 percent of all teenage arsonists are male
96 percent of the prison population is male

Report on the work of the Prison Service, 1991-2

42 percent of all female murder victims are killed by their male partner (9 percent of males are killed by their female partner)
48,000 children are now on the Child Protection Register
33 percent of all men born in the early 1950s have a criminal conviction. 21 percent of these for a violent crime.

Social Trends, 1993

Suicide is now the third most common cause of death in young people, after cancer and accidents. The Samaritans estimate that male suicide among under-25's went up by 50 percent between 1981 and 1991; a survey by the BBC program *Public Eye* put the figure at 86 percent. Typically, 4 out of 5 young suicide deaths will be male: between spring 1990 and spring 1991, 591 people under 25 killed themselves and only 79 were women.

Michele Elliot, director of Kidscape, believes that "boys do have new pressures. They are getting conflicting ideas about their role; what does being a man in the 1990s mean?"

Young people today feel they are tiptoeing across a minefield. Can they match up, be macho enough, be caring enough, be *enough?*

Annie Rankin, from "The Ballad of the Sad Young Men" in *The Sunday Times*, March 1, 1992

My guess is that these statistics will continue to grow until older men are prepared themselves to enter the minefield and help younger men deal with the explosives hidden in our culture.

In our recent past the industrial revolution took men out of the fields and away from their families to work in factories. At present we are in the middle of a technological revolution which is taking men out of the factory, putting some behind a computer, while many others become unemployed. With each shift, long-valued male qualities are edged out of play. Traditional strengths are no longer needed or valued. In particular, aggressive instincts—once not only essential for survival, but highly praised and desired—are now "out." But little has been done to make creative use of this energy. It will not disappear. It will find another door. Maybe the tragedies behind these statistics are this door.

As I began working with men on these and other issues, I was astonished by the similarity of male experience. Part of my isolation was caused by thinking I was alone; part of the healing occurred through realizing I was not. I learnt by simply being with and listening to other men in circumstances where the normal pressures to perform and succeed did not apply. One man's soulful reflections create a reservoir of images from which another can review his own experience. When a man says to me, "That happened to me, I know how you feel," I have found—however fleetingly—a brother.

MELTING THE STONE

My involvement was inspired by my family, or rather by my apparent inability really to be with my wife and children, even when I had the time and the inclination. I had to journey away from home, into groups of men, to face this distance within myself, and to learn a language in which I could express it. Every so often this ability to detach from life returns to haunt me, and my continuing work with men reminds me that it seems to come with the masculine territory. But when I can breach those defensive barriers then I am most alive. I can love my wife and children without embarrassment, and be with them without withdrawing emotionally. In those moments there is no masculine or feminine, just human beings loving each other as completely as possible.

Chapter One

The End of My Beginnings

It was 11:15 a.m., July 11, 1989. I was clearing up breakfast in the family cottage when my father's nurse came in and asked to speak to me outside. I followed him out of the room and away from my wife and sisters without suspicion, so when he turned and said, "It's happened . . . I'm sorry," for a moment I didn't know what he was talking about. But then I looked in his eyes and I knew. My father was dead.

I should have been with him. We had known for three days his death was coming and he had been unconscious for forty-eight hours. The family had attended him throughout, but at the actual moment of his death we were elsewhere. He was alone, save for the male nurse. Maybe he needed unfamilied solitude to let go his tenacious grip on life; maybe some karmic impulse was reflecting back to him the many times he was absent at important moments in our lives—I didn't know.

I stood in the corridor outside his room, trying to push such thoughts away. My father was dead, for Christ's sake, really. My heart skipped a beat, stood still for an instant of suspended time.

Then, almost imperceptibly, the world I had known for twenty-eight years shattered. I was suddenly filled with an awful elation. This was a moment I had been wanting and dreading, all my adult life. Some inner structure I had never been aware of was collapsing in upon itself, leaving me free, alone and terribly unprepared. An inner voice told me my life would never be the same again.

I moved towards the door of his room, my senses so heightened that my body moved in slow motion, as if wading through water. I approached the bed, watching his pale gray face growing in size, glowing in the gloomy room. I gazed at the motionless body searching for many things: confirmation, denial, a clue that he was just acting—still acting, a last blessing from father to son, a sign he was at peace . . .

I turned away and left the room—an uncomprehending childish part of me excited to be the bearer of such important news as I dashed about the house, gathering sisters, mother, wife, and baby son.

Soon we were all standing in his room, uncertain in the face of death: wanting to touch the man, fearful of disturbing the body. The women around me began to weep, softly, gently. I wanted to join them, wanted to prove I, too, had loved enough to cry. But I couldn't. I envied them. As I reached down inside, looking for something to release, something to offer the situation, I found only a stony wall and iron bars. I began feeling claustrophobic and became anxious to escape my awkwardness. When we left the room I breathed a long, guilty sigh of relief.

I headed for the phone, keen to continue being the messenger of death. I spoke in hushed, reverent tones, not quite sure if I was feeling it or acting it. Something else was taking over now, an efficient automatic pilot whom I could observe at work. As I ploughed through the long list of calls, I frequently felt tears spring up behind my eyes. These were not for my loss, they were in sympathy for the loss these friends felt. I was moved by the grief of others, yet unable to find my own.

By the time I had finished on the phone the doctor and funeral director had arrived. I avoided the room, unwilling to witness the body being manhandled, but followed them out to their car. My father was being carried in a curious fold-over sack—it was purple, his favorite color. I was amazed at how small the body bag seemed—as if the body had shrunk when his huge spirit had left. We arrived at the gate and the bundle was placed into the back of an aging Ford Cortina estate. The car drove off carefully but without dignity, up the bumpy farmtrack.

I looked at the leafy lane which was even now swallowing my father, and felt suddenly vulnerable. Some energy had left the grounds with my father's body; all invisible support that I had relied on and did not know how to replace. I shut and locked the gate. I returned to the house, made and put up NO ENTRY signs. I called our neighbors to ask that they lock a gate further down the lane, to stop any callers, especially the press. My father had always been generous with his house—Liberty Hall he would call it—my first actions as effective male head of this household were to close off, close down, be alone.

Later on I found myself leaning wooden trellises outside the kitchen door so the feared long-range lenses couldn't snap the Olivier household mess. The outward appearance would remain ordered, even if a human cost had to be paid for hiding the reality within. It had often been this way in my family life.

The rest of the day blazed by in manic practical activity; organizing the funeral, meeting our parish priest, fending off the press, and envisaging potential problems. That night was spent avoiding television news, family and close friends meeting in a series of huddles around the house. There was a struggle going on, in me at least, to keep the private man "alive" and to prevent public response from taking him away, perhaps for ever. Before retiring, I joined my sisters, Tamsin and Julie-Kate, upstairs in Dad's study. We laughed, talked, hugged, and reminisced, looking at old photos, remembering the good times, retelling favorite family tales. It was a kind of completion—or maybe a beginning—the first night we had known in this world without a father.

I went to bed, but couldn't sleep. I was unsure, unhinged. Dad had been ill, on and off, for fifteen years, suffering a variety of near crippling illnesses, each sapping a little more of his strength and vitality. For years I had been taking over more responsibility for his affairs and estate; in the recent past with little reference to him. But now, stripped of his physical presence, I felt like a little boy.

I woke early. I tried to fill the emptiness with a large breakfast, and ended up feeling slightly sick. For all my noble thoughts of privacy, I could no longer resist temptation, and as the newspapers arrived I read the reviews of my father's life—all good, most of them "raves," he would have approved.

One photograph caught my eye. It was on the front page of the *Independent*—a view of the National Theatre from across the river, its neon sign saying simply "Lord Olivier 1907-1989." In the foreground a couple, slightly out of focus, are apparently contemplating the sign. Of course, for all I knew they could have been discussing dog food; but in my fantasy they were thinking about him. A great man, part of our national artistic heritage had gone. For an instant I was with the couple, anonymous, never having met the man, yet somehow affected by his passing—aware that a chink of cultural armor had been lost. I drifted back from my reverie, faintly disturbed that my empathy with others was still more present than personal grief. I focused on organizing, well, anything really; I couldn't afford to feel more deeply.

The next two days, before the funeral, passed in a blur of excitement and panic. We went to the funeral parlor, to the church, and to the local police station—where, in my paranoid state, I managed to reverse the planned route of the funeral procession so we would not pass the press parking area on our way out. The amount of organization required for funerals may well be a necessary part of the process—life goes on, it doesn't just stop—but I welcomed the excuse to not even slow down. I made damn sure I did not have time to think about what and who I would be burying. I was content to be seen to be in control—the objective director, manipulating from the wings.

We decided to keep the funeral service intimate; family and close friends, no "political" invitations. My half-brother Tarquin and I would deliver the Bible readings, mine to be, "O Death, where is thy sting, Grave where is thy victory?" I assumed this would be quite simple. But as I paced around the garden reading it, I couldn't get to the end without my voice breaking, which really confused me. I was getting emotional about the imagined effect of my performance—"Wouldn't it be moving to see me read this . . ." —but not feeling anything in my own right. I felt a fake, as if my performance was more important to me than the funeral itself

I suddenly heard my father's words to me one honest, drunken night a decade before, "I don't know who I am—I've played two hundred characters in my life, and I know them all better than I know myself." It was probably this statement that had turned me away from acting. Yet here I was, living out my own weird version of this: "I don't know what I feel—though I feel what others will feel . . ." I had imagined that I had successfully moved away from him and his apparent "work over life" ethic. Maybe there was more of my father in me than I cared to admit.

The morning of Friday, July 14, heralded a perfect midsummer day, though everyone at home was nervous. The family would be on show at the funeral; no more hiding behind locked gates. We had been warned of "immense press interest," and we just had to lump it. Larry was a famous man, had played for his public all his life, and now if that public wanted a piece of him we would have to hand him over. My defenses rose as the hour approached. I had waged a silent war with this mythic public all my life, competing for affection. Today I had a premonition I would lose.

MELTING THE STONE

Our spirits cheered as friends arrived. Gawn Grainger, who was to read the main address, came up to ask advice. He was considering starting a round of applause at the end, a last curtain call for Larry, what did we think? I hesitated, caught between theatrical and religious ritual. (Oddly appropriate, as this was a lifelong struggle for my father, being the son of an Anglican priest.) Maybe people wouldn't join in, would it destroy the mood, what would the press think, was it disrespectful, too theatrical? I decided against it. Maybe I wanted to rob my father of a last round, maybe I just wanted the service to be about the man not the actor—I don't know. But the applause was cut.

Finally we loaded up and the cars set off for the small country church. I was in the front seat of the first car, heart pounding as we reached the police escort at the top of the lane, mouth drying as we crept through the nearby village. We turned the last corner—to be suddenly confronted by a wall of cameras opposite the church. They were carefully roped off so as not to physically prevent our progress; but no amount of rope could protect me from the freezing terror that gripped me as I gazed into that sea of lenses. Like the African tribesman who believes his soul may be captured in a photograph, I felt any genuine response I may have had at my father's funeral was being eroded by each closing shutter.

The car stopped. I hurried round to shield my mother, sisters, and wife as they emerged into the barrage. The situation was overwhelming. One hundred press on one side of the road, a hundred lenses pointing at our small group on the other. I'd seen this amount of cameras before, at awards ceremonies and premieres with my parents, but there it was part of the deal. Here it was absurd. We tried to ignore it, tried not to let them take away our dignity; they in turn tried not to shout, not to be disrespectful, but zooms zeroed in, waiting for a tear, a smile, a slip—a photo opportunity.

It seemed an age as the coffin was unloaded from the hearse and settled on the metal trolley required to push it over the cracked paving stones and under the low door into the church. The trolley reminded me of a hospital gurney. "Bit late for that"; my irreverent mind broke the ice. Our crown-shaped floral tribute was finally placed on top of the coffin and the bearers moved off with their load. Gratefully we followed it, away from the clicking crowd. Halfway down the path a trolley wheel slipped into a crack, the trolley lurched, the crown slid towards the edge of the coffin . . . then, miraculously, stopped. The trolley was readjusted and moved smoothly into the sanctity of the church. I breathed again. The nightmare headline—"Sir Larry: Uncrowned at Last!" —faded, though I was unaware it was the public not the private indignity I had most feared. We entered the cool, calm gloom, found our pews and sat down.

The service started and flowed around me, as I concentrated on maintaining equilibrium for my reading. Friends stood up and spoke with tender strength. I bit my lip, now determined not to give in, not to join their grief. Then I heard my cue.

I got to my feet, knees trembling. I focused on the lectern and followed my eyes, wading through the quicksand that rose from the stone floor and threatened to pull me down. I made it. I turned to look at the congregation, Bible clenched in my sweaty palm. Family, friends, faces I had known forever, pieces of the jigsaw puzzle that made up my father's life. Their eyes were filled with love, compassion, shared loss. I gulped for air, prayed for ghostly fathering and started to speak.

As the words tumbled out, part of me floated up above my body to observe myself below. But as I reached the familiar last lines, I plummeted down, acutely aware of Death and the Grave. My eyes stung with salt water. I swallowed hard, gritted my teeth and the words reluctantly followed. I faltered slightly on "Grave," giving out only at the end of "Victory." It was done. I shut the Bible and returned swiftly to my seat. I had survived without crying in public. The irony of refusing these tears while seeking others' did not strike me until long after.

The service ended with Larry's favorite hymn, "The King of Love my Shepherd Is," and we were herded out to the cars. Following our carefully laid plans, friendly Public Relations men now handed out press packets to delay attempts to follow us to the crematorium. These contained the readings and the last photograph I had taken of Larry, holding my son Troy, with the family motto underneath, "The Olive Tree flourishes, even as I rejoice in the House of the Lord." We had thought it appropriate; Troy flourishing while Larry (all being well) rejoiced upstairs. No one else seemed to get the connection, but the tactics worked. We slipped away to the crematorium unimpeded.

The second ceremony lacked the intense beauty of the church service. Travel and new surroundings broke the ritual mood; the simplicity of the ancient replaced by the high-tech design of the modern, complete with piped music and air conditioning. Even the words carried less weight than those I had tried to block out before. My spirits sank. I looked forward to the relative safety of the house.

At the wake I hid creeping depression behind a host's facade. I wandered around the garden, bottle in hand, escaping meaningful conversation. The memories of many other parties here with the same guests lent a curiously unreal quality to the proceedings. I half expected Dad to emerge from the house and be congratulated on another marvelous death scene. But not this time. I didn't know what I was feeling—it certainly wasn't what others assumed I was feeling—and I didn't want to be exposed as a fraud. I wove through the throng of familiar faces, harshly deciding which were friends and which had merely suffered my presence in order to be with a great man. Some I would never see again.

A story emerged from one group. A friend of the storyteller had been in a café in France when the news of Larry's death was announced. They had glanced at a calendar, and saw the day marked "St. Olivier's Day." Much wakelike jollity ensued—"The old fart always knew how to make an exit." I turned away, touched and distanced by the tale, towards where my fourteen-month-old son stood, small fingers pointing to the sky. I looked up to see an almost perfect "cross" of airplane vapor trails directly over the house and grounds.

The guests slowly drifted away. Vanloads of flowers arrived from the church and were placed around the lawn as the evening wore on. When the family gathered, my wife Shelley and I judged the time was right to announce the presence of another "olive branch." We had found she was pregnant only the day before we knew Dad was dying, and it hadn't felt right to mention it before. Such contradictory events were too much to take in together. But having sent Larry on his way, we now raised a glass to a future Olivier.

Later I slunk off; bearing a cigar, to sit alone, deeply grateful to have a birth to look forward to. I gazed at the stars interspersed here and there with landing lights approaching Gatwick, and images of my father began to roll up on an internal screen—a slide show gallery of our life together.

A huge murky figure in earliest childhood, not clear—pictures out of focus, somehow not present—a distance. A strange roughness of skin, occasional harshness of voice. Becoming softer, more approachable as the years rolled by, heavyset glasses an irresistible toy and a strange barrier to honest exchange. An awareness of a force that drew him out of the home, away from me. Learning not to miss him too much, for the missing never brought him back. Foreign holidays, playing with him in the sea, laughing for a while until some script drew him to it with more magnetic force than I seemed able to muster. At home a growing rebellion against female rule in his absence, leading to strict prep school. I feared him for sending me to this awful place. When he took me out for treats other people would stop him and talk to him, leaving me on the side, sometimes whole crowds pushing me out of the way to get his signature. And yet he listened, when he had time. He wanted me to go to Westminster School. We had visited there together; I had hated it—and he changed his mind. I went to board at Bedales instead. Now he was ill, had more time, would drive three hours to see me play sports against some strange school, while I was too embarrassed to talk to him at half-time, unable or unwilling to enjoy his effort. Another illness, and now I worried he would die.

The good times starting here too, traveling to film sets on holidays to be his assistant, friend, nurse. Protecting him from autograph hunters when he tired, exacting revenge on strangers for earlier times. Enjoying brushes with fame, storing tales of others' heroes to impress school mates. Loving him for providing this social ammunition, almost forgiving his age, his illnesses. Career advice, "Don't be a fucking actor . . . 92 percent unemployment," then when I told him I wanted to direct, "For God's sake act first. . . ." Trying to go to Oxford and please him, ending up at UCLA, his second choice. Vacation visits, grateful I didn't have to cope with his growing demands for family attention, now he was often too ill to work. His visits to me; coming to a fringe play I was in, at midnight, in downtown Hollywood, the day after his seventy-fifth birthday. Back in England attending every first night of mine he could, painfully edging into cars and being driven for hours to be there. No criticism now, just embarrassing praise. Almost silent dinners at home, struggling with failing memory, fading health. Moving in to the country cottage with him, to administer filial, impatient care. Waiting outside the hospital while he had his last, dangerous hip operation. Trying to inspire him to talk through unspoken fears about his life, in preparation for his death, and failing. Organizing an eighty-second birthday party with his close friends, sensing it may be his last. That gray face, rasping away for three days when lesser mortals would have given up the ghost. Coming briefly round to say, "I don't want this." Did he mean painful Life or impending Death?

I had flicked through these memory banks dispassionately. There were no obvious clues as to why this was, and some fear stopped me probing too deeply.

The next week oozed by in a heavy fog. I was trapped in the house surrounded by a lawnful of funeral flowers and tables full of consoling letters. Each message carried its own testimony of inspiration, adding new threads to the tapestry of my father's life. Friends, acquaintances, schoolteachers, doctors, actors, fans I had never met—some seeking signed photos. I felt proud reading them, until guilt stole in: how could they understand my loss better than me? Then I wanted to rewind the clock, break free, run away. But I had nowhere to go. And anyway, events conspired to render escape impossible. My father was no longer physically present, but I would spend the next three months intimately involved with his affairs.

Immediate concerns were the final resting place and a memorial service. The executors suggested approaching Westminster Abbey. A polite message was received back saying the Abbey would be delighted to host the memorial, but they had no room for the ashes. A couple of phone calls to St. Paul's Cathedral and we were able to pen a letter to the Abbey declining their kind offer as St. Paul's would be able to take ashes and service. The next day a message was biked back from the Abbey saying that an unfortunate error had occurred, the wrong person had received our first inquiry, and on further investigation space for the ashes had been found. Dad would have been tickled pink. The two greatest Anglican "theatres" in England were vying for his farewell performance, not to mention his earthly remains. But as the Abbey contained the triple attraction of the Shakespeare Memorial, King Henry V, and Larry's hero, Henry Irving, as potential new neighbors, we gratefully plumped for Westminster.

As the excitement died down and the planning started, I recalled my father's wish for me to go to Westminster School, next door to the Abbey. And my refusal. I had rejected the very place my father would now inhabit for ever. There were other ambitions he had for me that I had avoided: in sports, education, and career. Why was I so determined to reject his influence? A small inner voice was trying to be heard . . . but other louder voices quickly drowned it out, much to my relief.

It was a peculiar time. My father's death had been a very public affair, and everyone I met would remind me of it, while I was trying to forget. I wanted to get on as if nothing had changed, whereas in reality everything had changed; I simply was not able to see, accept, and act on these changes. A layer of parental protection, a psychic veil, had been stripped away, and I would have to face the world more closely. But instead of allowing time and space to adjust, I kept busy, over-organizing everything I could lay my hands on. Without realizing it, I was moving away from anything that exerted an emotional hold over me. I was on the run. And I made mistakes.

One memorable error was played out with an old friend of Larry's. We went to see Dustin Hoffman as Shylock in *The Merchant of Venice* and were all a little nervous, it being our first public family outing since the funeral. But backstage, in his dressing room, we soon relaxed, had a few drinks, spoke of Larry and laughed a lot. On our way out, full of confidence, I felt impelled to promise Dustin a memento of my father. He thanked me and I left. The next day, deeply moved by my inspiration and generosity, I carefully wrapped and posted the set of false teeth Dad had worn as Shylock twenty years before. I relished my impeccable logic. Larry and Dustin had worked together on *Marathon Man*—their most memorable scenes together connected with teeth. Larry had only "discovered" how to play Shylock when he wore these false teeth. They were a piece of National Theatre history! How appropriate for Dustin to inherit them, now he was playing Shylock. I was so impressed with the idea that I never bothered to imagine its effect. I still cringe with embarrassment when I think of him unwrapping the box, expecting a treasured token and finding . . . gnashers! I never heard from him—I'm not surprised.

This suppression of common sense and instinct spread its influence. Over-logical career choices led to other mistakes. I had agreed to direct a new play and was discussing rewrites. There was something about the project that didn't feel quite right, and Shelley would be due to deliver our new baby the week rehearsals started. My mind overruled such unreasonable objections; "It'll be fine," it said. My first West End show, *Shirley Valentine*, had opened a couple of weeks before Dad died, and looked set to be a success. "So you can tackle anything now . . ." it lied. An internal imbalance was gradually being reflected outwardly. And I refused to see it, relying on work to keep me on an even keel.

The irony was that the very work I was doing to avoid an emotional response to my father's death revolved exclusively around him. I was running his estate, helping deal with his will, preparing for the memorial service at Westminster Abbey, planning a tribute evening at the National Theatre and helping to compile a book, *Olivier at Work—The National Years.* Even after his death I was putting more energy into his affairs than my own.

Of all these projects the national tribute was the one I was most directly responsible for, and, appropriately enough, was the only one to be abandoned. Early outrageous ideas included: Diana Ross singing Noël Coward, Jack Lemmon and Lauren Bacall in *Long Day's Journey into Night,* reuniting the *Beyond the Fringe* team, Dustin Hoffman as Shylock (he'd already got the teeth, hadn't he?) and an appearance of the man himself, courtesy of his hologram from the musical *Time.*

The only way to have raised a big enough budget would have been with television interest and sponsorship. But after a few cool responses, Joan and I got cold feet. We had no wish to push tributes that were deemed unnecessary. When the project was "indefinitely postponed," I found myself deeply relieved. I had been caught between pride in his achievements and guilt at possibly being seen as promoting myself at his expense.

Patrick Garland had agreed to be artistic supervisor for the Abbey memorial service, which left family and executors free to concentrate on the seemingly endless stream of administrative details and political considerations. On advice invitations were eventually extended to most of the Royal Family—but initially we concerned ourselves with those we thought Larry would have wanted there. Not the Queen—after she had dozed off during the play that opened the "new" National Theatre, Dad had always firmly stated that "She would rather look at the back end of a horse than a play." (This view was perhaps confirmed by Prince Edward, who told a National Youth Theatre charity crowd that when he had complained to his mother, "You don't know what it's like working a hard day in the theatre . . ." she had replied, "Oh, yes, I do . . . I go to the Royal Variety Show every year.") Not Prince Philip, whom Larry had never forgiven for calling the National Theatre "an awful concrete block" to his face. Prince Charles was invited (Larry luckily having missed his description of the National), as was the Queen Mother and Prince Edward.

The tension rose as the replies came in. Prince Edward would be granted royal dispensation from Sir Andrew Lloyd Webber; the Queen Mother would be in Scotland but would send a representative; Prince Charles was unavailable but had asked Kenneth Branagh to represent him. According to Royal protocol, the representative carries the same position in etiquette as the Royal he or she represents. Therefore, as the invitations stood, Mr. Branagh— as senior Royal representative—would be the last person to enter the Abbey. He would be met at the door and escorted by the Dean, while the entire congregation, including Prince Edward, stood until he was seated. Frankly, I think several surviving senior Thespians would have passed away on the spot. Moreover, those close to Larry knew him to be not entirely selfless and to have gone to the grave firmly clutching whatever laurels he had earned. The last thing he'd want at his memorial would be the apparent crowning of an heir to his throne.

But how do you tell the heir to the real throne that he had made a mistake? We were saved by a bell from the Renaissance Company office, who called to ask advice. I explained our concern about what the press would make of the situation, and its potential to detract from the event's primary purpose. The danger was understood, and Sir Richard Attenborough became a welcome, press-safe, Royal representative.

But as the immediacy of this threat faded, other questions rose up. Here was a young man, of my generation, ambitious and talented enough to challenge for a crown which I, as son of the king, had abdicated any interest in. Why had I run away from the spotlight? In the back of my mind grew the suspicion that my decision had been based on simple cowardice—a terror of trying and being seen to fail. Had I allowed that fear to grow so much that it had stopped me from ever trying? Did I lack the courage to step into the firing line, or was it genuinely not the right firing line for me to step into? Help, an identity crisis question—with no answer.

The memorial loomed. Tension rose as the sheer scale of the event became evident: live television and radio broadcast; royalty, ambassadors, politicians, and every actor I had ever heard of currently in the country. The thought that all this was for Dad was mindboggling.

The day before, I went to the Abbey for a televised interview, vaguely aware I was being used by the BBC to help attract a TV audience for the next day, and not being able to figure out if I minded. I passed through the main building, where Patrick Garland was rehearsing tomorrow's readers, and entered the small courtyard where the camera crew had set up. I chatted through the proposed questions, feeling relaxed. When asked to sum up how Larry would feel about the event, I said that whenever he entered a church he worried that the roof would fall on his head. I turned to the scaffolding around the Abbey and finished, "It looks as if he was right!" The interviewer said that was fine and now we'd go through it again on tape.

They started recording and I froze. I attempted to regurgitate the conversation but it felt stilted, cold, calculated; with a mean, self-aggrandizing finish. The difference between the "rehearsal" and the "performance" was stark. I now felt as if I was lying, whereas in reality I was simply pretending to be spontaneous. Ironically, the real subject of the interview had spent his entire life "lying" in just this way. Why did it make me so uncomfortable?

MELTING THE STONE

I retreated to the Abbey alone with my thoughts. I sat in Poets' Corner, imagining what it would be like when my father's ashes eventually lay under my feet. Suddenly his voice boomed out at me. I jumped, fearing for a terrible millisecond I had awakened the dead. Until I heard the youthful tones in the voice, recognized the St. Crispin's Day speech from *Henry V* and remembered the family decision to allow Dad one last chance to upstage his mates.

It was the first time I had heard his voice since he died. It felt like some weird exhumation. His work would live on. A selfish voice complained that here was proof that he would go on pleasing the public long after he could do anything for me. The tape replayed its passionate exhortation:

> We few, we happy few, we band of brothers;
> For he today that sheds his blood with me
> Shall be my brother . . .
> And gentlemen in England now a-bed
> Shall think themselves accurs'd they were not here,
> And hold their manhood's cheap; whiles any speak
> That fought with us upon St. Crispin's day.

(William Shakespeare, *Henry* V, Act IV Scene 3)

As the crescendo of sound echoed round those ancient walls, I suddenly saw this "band of brothers" as actors, those who shed sweat and blood on the stage. I was excluded from this brotherhood; as a director, I was hiding "a-bed in England." And, yes, I did hold my manhood cheap in the reverberation of his vocal power. He would not yet rest quietly in the grave, he was still speaking to me, haunting me, taunting me for my cowardice. I went home, trying not to worry about the day ahead. And, not for the first time, wondering along what path my manhood lay.

The memorial itself was a beautiful, stunning tribute. There was little room for "Dad" on this day, this was for "Lord Olivier O.M. Actor." I was inspired and overawed by the majesty of the occasion, feeling simultaneously an important part of his life and an unimportant part of his achievements. As I walked through the congregation of two thousand people—all of whom had felt their lives touched by his—and as the participants stood, one after another, to offer their tributes, I was caught in the contrary extremes of pride and shame. I felt so honored to be his son and so aware of how little I measured up in comparison.

The Dean spoke the bidding:

On Friday, October 20, 1905, Sir Henry Irving was buried in Poets' Corner. Eighty-four years later to the day we come to honor the greatest actor of our time; and next year the ashes of Laurence Olivier will lie beside those of Irving and Garrick, beneath the bust of Shakespeare, and within a stone's throw of the graves of Henry V and The Lady Anne, Queen to Richard III.
Laurence Olivier received from God a unique and awesome talent which he used to the full. We come then to give thanks:

for his integrity and professionalism;
for his magnetism, his powers of observation, his boldness and his sense of danger;
for his breathtaking versatility and his combination of strength and grace;
for his resilience and his incorrigible sense of humor;
for his courage, both as an actor and in facing illness and pain, and for so long outfacing death;
and for the joy he found at the end in his garden and in the love of his family.

Non Nobis Domine: Not unto us, O Lord, but unto thy name give the praise.

The words "tough act to follow" drifted lazily through my mind. While one part of me basked in the reflected glory, another darker part was telling me I would never match up. There were two worlds existing in my head simultaneously. One wanting to go on as before, another demanding change, blood and death. But a death of what? Maybe a clue lay in John Mills's reading:

> When I was a child, I spake as a child, I understood as a child, I thought as a child; but when I became a man, I put away child-ish things . . .
>
> (I Corinthians 13)

How? All I knew was how childish I felt that day, the child of a great man, needing to look for something that I did not have. And not knowing where to start.

Sir Alec Guinness finished his address saying, "There may be many imitators but there is no second Olivier; he was unique." I felt again the familiar urge to run away from the challenge of being an Olivier. It seemed only half my name was my own—Olivier wholly owned by Laurence. I thought of an article about Michael Douglas which referred to Kirk Douglas as "Michael's acting fa-ther." I doubted I would ever read an Olivier equivalent, and cursed myself for caring.

The service finished with a glorious trumpet fanfare, and we were wafted out on a wave of excited emotion. We drove to the reception at the National Theatre, where doubts were fueled by the appearance of each successive, successful guest. Would I really ever match up in their eyes to my father? And was this to be my life, trying and inevitably failing to overcome a myth and "beat" my father on his own territory? I prowled around the reception wondering how I could escape the shadow I felt threatening my very existence. Now the official tributes were over and public duty done, I was determined to escape from it. What I did not see was how much else of value I would have to leave behind.

Chapter Two

A Short Sharp Shock

In the months after my father's death I lost myself in a crowded schedule, maintaining my isolated position. Of course it was not just this event, major though it was, that had sent me into permafrost. I was to realize later that this had been the catalyst, a moment of critical mass that had activated a defensive reaction set up many years ago. And, indeed, the kind of reaction that could be classified as "typically masculine." I had pulled in my antennae and battened down the hatches. I dare not trust anyone, especially those closest to me. For those with whom I should have had an intimate relationship became those who posed the greatest threat. Anyway, I imagined my wife Shelley must have quite enough to do looking after our son, and herself. I did not wish to burden her with my *Angst,* and I did not know how to begin. I had no vocabulary to start a conversation, no language to express the lack of emotion I felt at the core of my being. I manufactured a brave face that said everything would be fine . . . tomorrow. Or soon. And wondered why I felt a fake.

MELTING THE STONE

The first time I caught sight of the tip of this iceberg, it was a shock. A good friend, Jackie Leven, gave me a recording of a poetry reading by the American poet Robert Bly. I had ignored poetry since leaving my last English Literature class many years before, fed up with the intellectual game of interpretation and dissection. This was the first time I could remember hearing poems read by the poet, performed for the heart not the brain.

One of them managed to creep under the battlements:

A MAN WRITES TO A PART OF HIMSELF

What cave are you in, hiding, rained on?
Like a wife, starving, without care,
Water dripping from your head, bent
Over ground corn . . .

You raise your face into the rain
That drives over the valley—
Forgive me, your husband,
On the streets of a distant city, laughing,
With many appointments,
Though at night going also
To a bare room, a room of poverty,
To sleep beside a bare pitcher and basin
In a room with no heat—
Which of us two then is the worse off?
And how did this separation come about?

(from the *Selected Poems of Robert Bly*)

As these words filtered down I saw a brief image of myself, split into these two parts. That small voice, which I had occasionally heard over the last months and had resolutely dismissed, piped up again, more insistent now, "Yes, I am this other, this 'wife'; this is me, and you ignore me at your peril." I allowed myself to travel with this voice, and found myself in his far-away cave. It was stony

36

and dry. No heat, no warmth, no love. And then, as if looking through a telescope in a dream, I saw the everyday Richard Olivier, far-away, busy, "laughing with many appointments." A chill wind blew around both bodies, as if to remind them of their separation.

And I saw then how I must be starving Shelley of care as well. It was not deliberate, but I had no food to give. I was too hungry myself to take care of others. This inability to give to those I loved was deeply disturbing. But a small glimmer of hope was soon to be offered. Before I could completely forget my disquiet, Jackie told Shelley and me that Robert Bly was coming to England soon to lead a couple of workshops, one with his wife Ruth on relationships, the other, for men—"Male Initiation and the Grief of its Absence." We were suitably intrigued and both signed up for the first, me for the second.

And so, a few weeks after the memorial, Shelley and I arrived outside a small hall in Hampstead for the workshop elusively titled, "Desire, the Egg and the Royal Pair. . . ." As we parked I began to feel nervous. I had never done anything like this before; assuming that a relationship was what you were in, what you worked on was your career. Even showing up was a confession of failure, wasn't it?

We walked in and introduced ourselves to the organizers, Noel Cobb and Eva Loewe. I calmed down, they seemed happy enough, and sane. Maybe I didn't have to feel so bad just being here. There were about forty of us gathering under the auspices of the "London Convivium for Archetypal Studies." (I knew where London was—the rest was a mystery.) I settled in my chair and looked cautiously around, quickly growing suspicious of some aging hippies chatting in another corner. If this was a "we can have peace and love—even under Thatcher" weekend, I was leaving.

But it wasn't—and I didn't. Robert and Ruth Bly came in. He was older than I imagined, in his early sixties, with a shock of white hair, an exuberant, large frame and a multicolored vest. Ruth was younger and more considered in appearance. They worked well together, basing the day around a Norwegian fairy tale called "White Bear—King Valemon," and deftly teasing out poetic and psychological images from the story.

From the beginning I experienced a strange mixture of relaxation and excitement. The words and images were striking bells inside my body that had been silent for a long time. It was fascinating to be drawn into the world of a fairy tale, the kind of story I had abandoned early on in my life, and yet to find there insights into my current situation. It was the first time I had "given myself up" to a story like this.

Later I found confirmation of this strange capacity in *The Uses of Enchantment—the meaning and importance of fairy tales*, by Bruno Bettelheim:

> Fairy stories represent in imaginative form what the process of healthy human development consists of . . . more can be learned from them about the inner problems of human beings, and of the right solutions to their predicaments in any society than from any other type of story . . . Through the centuries (if not millennia) during which, in their retelling, fairy stories became ever more refined, they came to convey at the same time overt and covert meanings—came to speak simultaneously to all levels of the human personality, communicating in a manner which reaches the uneducated mind of the child as well as that of the sophisticated adult . . .
>
> (from pages 5 and 12)

These tales act as storehouses of ancient knowledge but remain fluid because they require the imagination to "water them" into life. They are not fixed to a single interpretation: they are able to hold different meanings for different people, and can even have different meanings for the same person at different times. A good story becomes an "image magnet"—the conscious mind will be attracted to the image that has most to say to us at that time. The event in the tale that strikes us acts as a doorway to lead us to the part of the psyche that requires attention. It is a metaphor for the stage of life we are going through.

That day the story of "White Bear—King Valemon" was viewed as a metaphor for our relationships. In brief, the tale went like this:

One day a Princess was walking in the forest when she saw a great white bear playing with a golden wreath. She was so taken with the beauty of the wreath that she asked the bear if she could have it. She offered anything he wished in return. He replied he wished her hand in marriage. Despite her father's objections they were married, and went off to live in the bear's castle, where the bear would become a man during the night. They lived happily for three years, during which time the Princess gave birth to three children, all of whom disappeared. The Princess began to miss her parents and asked to visit them. The bear gave his permission, warning her not to listen to what her mother said. Her mother doubted her story and urged the Princess to light a candle to see the bear at night. When the Princess did so, she saw a beautiful man. But he woke up appalled to see the light, and changing back into a bear, started to leave. The Princess hung onto his fur, but was dragged through brambles and bushes, and eventually fell off. She wanders through the forest for years, alone, searching for the White Bear King Valemon.

Eventually she arrives at a hut with an old woman and a little girl. She plays with the girl who asks if she may give the Princess a magic flask, which will pour out whatever the owner desires. The Princess visits two more huts where she plays with children and is given a magic tablecloth and scissors, which provide endless food and cloth. She is directed to a glass mountain on which Valemon is said to live. At the bottom she finds a hut full of starving children. She feeds them, and their father, a blacksmith, forges iron claws so she can climb the mountain.

But Valemon is due to marry a witch in three days. She uses her gifts to bargain with the witch to spend each night in Valemon's room. The first two nights the witch drugs Valemon, and the Princess can only cry all night, next to him. On the third day two carpenters who sleep next to Valemon's room tell him they heard crying. This night Valemon avoids the sleeping draught and sees the Princess again. They make their plans, dispose of the witch, pick up the three children from the old women's huts, and marry as King and Queen.

The first stage we called "The Promise of the Golden Wreath." This was like the initial throes of romantic love: golden and full of magical promise. This blissful state sweeps the couple off their feet, makes their previous lives pale in comparison, carries them through the wedding, the honeymoon, and into the early months or years of marriage. So far so good. But something, maybe, is being avoided. The babies are disappearing, and no one is saying anything.

It was suggested that this is a necessary but unrealistic phase. Literally it is too good to be true. In real life we may feel like our partner is a "dream," but eventually we have to accept that they (like us) are not perfect. The longer we try to keep up the pretense that everything is great simply because we love each other, the more "babies" will disappear.

The energy created by being in love takes us out of our parents' grasp and propels us towards our own life. In the beginning there may be a sensation that "I know you completely, instantly," which is a nice idea but patently untrue. It is, more likely, an image we have invented of an ideal partner that we project onto the face and person of a real human being. They may be flattered by the adoration they receive and agree to go around holding this ideal image for us to enjoy, for a while. But eventually something is going to crack. At some point you wake up from the dream and have to deal with the reality:

(excerpt from) LISTENING TO THE KÖLN CONCERT

When men and women come together,
how much they have to abandon! Wrens

make their nests of fancy threads
and string ends, animals

abandon all their money each year.
What is that men and women leave?
Harder than wren's doing, they have
to abandon their longing for the perfect.

The inner nest not made by instinct
will never be quite round,
and each has to enter the nest
made by the other imperfect bird.

(from *Robert Bly—Setected Poems)*

The story seems to say, we must go back before we can go on, find out about the nest we came from, our parents' house. But it is not easy; the crack in the relationship widens following a visit to the parents. It is as if we begin to see our partner with our parents' eyes. Inherited habits, temporarily overcome in the flush of romantic love, may now return and cast a harsh light on our mysterious ideal image. We begin to see through the projection, take off our rose-tinted glasses—and the feeling of the other's "perfection" fades.

After the "honeymoon" period the intense energy that brought a couple together turns towards new family life and responsibilities. But the temptation is for each partner to impose their old family habits on this new life. They bring a candle given to them by their parents into the marital home and shine it on their spouse. An invisible battle is fought between the different families of origin, armed with different backgrounds. Without realizing it, each partner wants the other to want what they want, do what they do, in the way that they do it. Our first lesson on relationships came from watching our parents, and we will have inevitably picked up (at least some of) their habits. This early training will keep returning, until or unless we become aware of it. Only then can we start to unravel it.

But both these early stages are biased, the first towards naive dreams and blind love, the second towards doubt and criticism. The first says, "You are perfect and perfect for me," the second, in essence, says, "Why can't you be more like my mother (or father)?" Since neither of these will work for long, we move on to the next stage, "Falling Apart." I was beginning to get uneasy.

Here the world provides excuses for each to turn away from the other. The brambles of life scratch at the skin until the one has to let go the clinging attachment to the other. Traditionally the man will turn to work and duty, the woman to home and family in search of the fulfillment the partner no longer provides. (This pattern may be changing, but the divorce rate indicates the "falling apart" is still buried under other interests rather than faced within the relationship.) Most couples are not aware of, or prepared for, the painful journey between the youthful idealism of the Prince and Princess and the hard-earned maturity of the King and Queen.

As each stage became apparent I had to suppress a groan of recognition. I had met Shelley in America, fallen deeply in love, felt my life change overnight and got married. Three months later we came to England for a visit and ended up living in my parents' house. Anxious to forge a career I had turned to work while Shelley was left to fashion whatever home she could within my father's country cottage. It had all seemed so natural, so inevitable, but I had failed to see that in doing this we had already "fallen apart." The energy that had previously gone into my marriage was now used exclusively outside it, to keep going, to keep building, to keep running. Shelley had to direct her energy to Troy, to the coming baby, to maintaining the home. Somewhere along the line I had stopped seeing her as a Princess, and she had stopped seeing me as a Prince. I had become a director, she a mother. We had both been disappointed by the change but had lost the intimacy we needed to talk about it.

According to the story this disappointment is inevitable; it will happen, at some time, in every relationship. If we can recognize it we have a chance to work with it, and to search for what is missing. If we do not recognize the disappointment it will grow into a sense of betrayal. There was an implied promise that the golden wreath will last forever, "This feeling will never end." But it has; the gold is gone, the promise broken.

Since it was not deliberate, we feel innocent and blame the other, silently saying, "I haven't changed so it must be your fault." They failed to live up to the ideal image we threw upon them. But blame blocks the intimacy that could heal it. It was created by a realization of distance, "You are different from what you were," (which should read "You are different from the way I imagined you to be") and creates more distance.

The very space that was once brimming with love fills with rejection. This will stimulate old memories of childhood abandonment. The ideal image is replaced with the terrible, and new projections aimed at the partner contain old anger, resentment, even hate. The Princess turns into the evil Witch, the Prince into the cannibalistic Giant. Without anything definable going wrong, a vicious circle has developed. One feels less loved, becomes disappointed, blames the other, gets angry, gives less—so the other feels less loved . . . etc., etc., "ad divorcum."

I felt another shock wave of recognition. I looked at Shelley, and felt, briefly, the sadness of this falling apart and of the distance there seemed to be between us. Coming here had not been a fortuitous accident, we had both known something was up, but had been unable to figure out what it was. We were too close to it, and needed to keep up appearances in order to function. But now we were on the verge of this next stage, trying to stop the disappointment turning into attack. But were we in time?

Those who felt themselves in this position were asked to consider the question:

What am I going to do about this ungodly need I feel in every cell in my body that is *not* going to be met by my partner?

43

This was a tough one, made only slightly easier by knowing it applied to others too. If it had been just me I think I would have found a way to avoid the question. For the first time I had to admit that there was this kind of driving need inside of me.

Then I saw how I had expected Shelley to meet this need. We had struck an unspoken deal whereby she would take care of my emotional stuff. I would do the thinking, maybe for both of us, she would do most of the intuiting and all of the feeling. Because she seemed so good at it, I had joyfully imagined she could make up for my lack. Of course my demons had not revealed themselves to her until safely after the wedding day, but there had been an assumption that she could take care of them. After all they had kept quiet during the intense period of our courtship. Surely this was "proof" that being with Shelley should be enough. This was the first time I had considered that it wasn't, and shouldn't be. They were my responsibility. I felt suddenly alone, vulnerable, and outnumbered.

This, appropriately enough, was where our separated lovers in the story were, too. Wandering through the forest, gaining magic by suffering and solitude. As Ruth Bly said—with total conviction and more than a little glee, "You are going to be alone, whether you are married or not." Which didn't make me feel any better.

The first task was to recognize the separation, then put it to good use. This would mean breaking the vicious circle of blame and anger in the relationship. As long as we put the blame on another we are able to avoid entering the forest. If we can see the blame as blame, rather than righteous indignation at the other's "failings," we can start to take it back. As D. H. Lawrence put it:

INTIMATES

Don't you care for my love? she said bitterly.

I handed her the mirror, and said:
Please address these questions to the proper person!
Please make all requests to head-quarters!
In all matters of emotional importance
Please approach the supreme authority direct! —
So I handed her the mirror.

To look in the mirror is to see ourselves. To wander lonely in the forest is to be by ourselves, with no one else to blame. If we stay there long enough we may find our anger and sense of betrayal comes more from within than without. Then we can start to work with our own limitations, rather than seeing them only in our partner.

The needs we previously placed on the other may come from us, from our parents or from our childhood. The children in the story are the neglected, lost children from the marriage; and the magic gifts are earned by paying attention to them. So we must pay attention to the neglected childish parts of us, to earn the magic that can meet the "ungodly need."

The time in the forest is not a literal separation in the physical world, but the mutual acknowledgment that both partners have their own stuff to work on, for a while. Each needs to go into a dark secluded place; to separate the wood from the trees and to sort out the fertilizer from the toxic waste.

As the event drew to a close I was aware of a tingling sensation in my stomach, as if something was trying to wake up, after years of sleep, urging me towards the forest. In some ways it was a relief to know I could go, in fact had to go, alone. Before it would have felt like more of a failure; "this relationship isn't working so I've got to be alone" would have felt like another excuse not to deal with it. And Shelley may have felt she had failed because I did not want her to come along for this particular ride, and that we would both be driven further apart by the remedy. But in the terms of the story it was inevitable; not a failure but simply another phase. And a phase that both partners had to undergo, but which would lead towards a greater bond. The union of King and Queen could never happen without going through the forest.

I left the building in a curious state of terrified inspiration. Excited by the knowledge that anything would be better than the slippery slope of inactivity, but scared that I might change and not recognize the stranger who came back. Maybe I would find a clue, or at least some more courage, at the upcoming men's workshop.

Chapter Three

The Third Man

The next Saturday I drove with Jackie Leven to Victoria for an event called "Male Initiation and the Grief of its Absence." On the way I asked him where he had first come across Robert Bly. He was silent for a moment, and then said at school. He had been expelled, but the local authority had insisted he be allowed back on the grounds that there was nowhere else to send him. This the headmaster grudgingly accepted, on the strict condition that no one talk to him, neither pupils nor teachers. As a result, Jackie had spent a year "in Coventry," alone, in the school library. In order to survive he had instinctively made his way to the poetry section. He stayed there, working his way through the lot. The poet whose work with alienation and depression had spoken most directly to him had been Robert Bly. In some way, he felt, he owed his sanity to Robert. We spent the rest of the ride in silence.

We parked and walked through the deserted business district, now wondering aloud what lay before us. We were both nervous, and substantially more so than we had been the previous week-end. Even the idea of meeting only with other men seemed dangerous. Jackie's associations with all male groups ranged from street gangs in Fife, working in a whisky factory, through a rock and roll band, and into the London drug scene. None of these had inspired him with trust. My associations were less dramatic, if more middle class: boarding-school bullying, aggressive sports, and a wild, homophobic fringe theatre company in Los Angeles. On second thoughts maybe we both had cause to be nervous.

We entered a gray concrete building and were directed down to the windowless basement. We half-heartedly greeted the few men we recognized from the couples workshop, but already a very different atmosphere prevailed. Gone was the *bonhomie* of the week before, replaced by an uneasiness, a more explicit threat. Men stood around, backs to the walls, sizing up potential friends and foes across the room. The weekend before we could pretend it was all the wife's idea, nothing to do with us. This time we were here alone, for a reason. Something must be wrong. It was embarrassing that our very presence implied this to other men.

Suddenly a small, wiry looking man came up to me. He had a ponytail and dancing eyes. He gave me a brochure for a men's workshop he was leading out in the wild, then urged me to look at some photographs he had taken of the last one. As I flicked through them and saw mostly naked men lying on rocks and holding each other, I felt a cold chill run down my spine. I wanted to leave the room, escape from this man and his pictures. An unspoken fear of touchy-feely exercises with homo-erotic overtones had just become reality. If this was what men's groups were about I wouldn't be staying past opening time.

I turned to Jackie for confirmation: I wasn't going insane, was I? Some bastard had just done a number on us, hadn't he? Jackie agreed. We reassured each other that he was nothing to do with the organizers or with Robert Bly, moved to the other side of the room and sat down quickly, before our fears got the better of us.

Robert Bly came in and settled down. He, too, was in a different mood than before, less colorful in attire, with stronger, more determined physical movements. He spoke with a harder edge, as if to say, "OK, this is going to be tough, but somebody's got to do it."

We settled down, grateful to have a focus for our anxiety, and listened to a poem:

I AM NOT I

I am not I.
        I am this one
Walking beside me that I do not see,
Whom at times I manage to visit,
And at other times I forget.
The one who forgives, sweet, when I hate,
The one who remains silent when I talk,
The one who takes a walk when I am indoors,
The one who will remain standing when I die.

(Juan Ramon Jiminez, translated by Robert Bly)

In this setting, in the company of these thirty men, I had, briefly, a real sense of this other "I." He was a possibility that existed for me, someone who could fill the emptiness inside. Indeed it may be his absence that caused the emptiness in the first place. If this indistinct sensation was the shape of the man I could become, I had not yet journeyed very far towards him.

We were asked to introduce ourselves and say why we had come. Here was another test. We would slip into the outer world game of competition, see who could come up with the best answer, or would we keep it honest? Perhaps inevitably it was a mixture. A few men, the compulsive "bosses," tried to be impressive with convoluted psychological theories that seemed to tell the rest of us how to live. But most were self-effacing, reticent about speaking of private concerns publicly. I was a raw beginner, unsure of the form. I muttered something about my father dying—no names, of course—and, feeling stuck, sat down as soon as possible. Even this had felt like a performance; when it was over I could breathe a bit more, and listen.

I found myself being slowly drawn in to a surprisingly generous sympathy. As tales of divorce, separation and death, violent or
absent fathers, possessive mothers, and breakdowns were presented
to the room, a lingering distrust of these strange men evaporated.
The sharing of pain and loss managed to undercut the fear. Tension dissolved, to be replaced by a tentative, silent community
drawn together by the common thread that echoed beneath the
spoken word: "There's something missing in my life as a man, I
know it, I feel it, and I don't know what to do about it. . . ."

For many, including myself, it was the first time I had heard
strangers talk in this way, particularly men. I knew no men I would
have felt comfortable talking with like this. Even with close friends
there was a "no-go area," a subtle line that we did not cross.

I once asked Willy Russell why he had written *Shirley Valentine*
from a woman's point of view. He replied that it was essential that
his character be able to talk about failure and loss. In his experience women talk and laugh openly about failure—what went
wrong, why, how, and with whom; while men talk and laugh about
success—victories, scores, promotions. He didn't think a man could
talk with the same emotional honesty. The psychologist Sam Keen
gives good reasons for this:

> Silence is manly, and we are trained to keep our feelings inside.
> Better a heart attack than speaking openly about a broken heart
> . . . we have been so conditioned to curtail our natural needs for
> intimacy that only in sex do we have cultural permission to feel
> close to another human being. . . . Emotionally speaking, men
> are stutterers who often use sexual language to express their
> forbidden desires for communion. What else would you expect
> from a gender that has been trained for generations to be war-
> riors and workers and conditioned not to feel or express but to
> stand and deliver?
>
> (*Fire in the Belly,* p. 78)

But if some of the old male roles were changing, could men change
and become more emotional? And was this a good thing?

The defining masculine energies of our ancestors—in particular the hunter, the soldier, the aggressor, and the provider—are no longer valued. The hunter is demonstrated against, the soldier accused of murder, the aggressor on the street is imprisoned (while his boardroom equivalent gets a bonus), and the provider is mocked by radical feminists and the media. The menu of male identity has been stripped of the old essential ingredients, but new positive recipes have not yet been created.

Robert Bly argued that in the 1960s men turned to the "feminine" in an attempt to change old habits. The Hippie culture was a move towards a more nurturing sensibility, conventionally associated with women. While plenty of old-style males still strutted their stuff, the "new man" tried to compensate for them, becoming more thoughtful and gentle. In the 1970s these feminine values became the new ideal, evidenced by the growth of Women's Liberation and the emergence of what Bly called "the soft male":

> Lovely, valuable people—not interested in harming the earth or starting wars. But many of these men are not happy. You quickly notice the lack of energy in them. They are life preserving, but not exactly life giving. Ironically you often see these men with strong women who positively radiate energy . . .
>
> (*Iron John: A Book About Men*, p. 3)

The gender pendulum swung towards the feminine. But as women found their voice and became more active, men seemed to lose theirs and turn passive. This may have been a necessary step, but it should not be mistaken for the end of the journey. A better relationship might be between an active woman and an active man—neither passive.

I felt that I fitted into the "soft male" mold. With my father generally away working, I had been brought up in a houseful of women; mother, nanny, housekeeper, and two sisters. I had been taught to temper my aggression, had learnt to value my sensitivity, but felt cornered and suffocated. I wanted an active man around, but failing that, yearned to get out. I ended up at boarding school—but that's another story.

Recently women have voiced dissatisfaction with the "soft male." Along with the domination and violence, positive energies were also suppressed. Somehow in trying to rid himself of his old dangerous activity, the soft male also lost his passion, his imagination, and his sense of adventure—which are precisely the qualities necessary to move ahead.

As John Guare writes in *Six DegTees of Separation:*

> One of the great tragedies of our times is the death of the imagination. Because what else is paralysis?
> I believe that the imagination is the passport we create to take us into the real world. [It] is another phrase for what is most uniquely us.
> To face ourselves. That's the hard thing. The imagination [is] God's gift to make the act of self examination bearable. [It] teaches us our limits and how to grow beyond our limits. [It] is not our escape. On the contrary, the imagination is the place we are all trying to get to . . .

The use of imagination in our culture has been waning for a long time, and is related to the loss of mythology. The Age of Reason decided that everything could be explained, psychology decided that everything could be analyzed, and television decided that everything could be shown. We rely on a select few artists to be imaginative for us, and end up watching game shows. Joseph Campbell said that what we learn in myth is about ourselves as part of the world. Mythology has the power to seize the soul, awaken it, and fill it with images. But if the imagination is dead, there is no receptacle for these images. Mythology dries up, "myth" becomes another word for fake. And we lose the sense that we are part of the world. If we can regain this sense we may be able to create a passport to the future. First we would have to re-educate ourselves not to rely only on the rational world view—but to try to incorporate a mythological perspective.

This was something we were attempting, courtesy of an ancient fairy tale, "Iron John." The tale was told in segments—this version condensed from "Jack of Iron," number 136 in the *Complete Grimm's Fairy Tales,* and Robert Bly's translation in *Iron John—A Book About Men.*

Once there was a King who lived in a castle. There was a great forest near this castle which had a bad reputation—whoever went in did not return. Many hunters disappeared there, and whole platoons of soldiers. Soon no one went into the forest. A long time passed, until one day a fearless hunter from another land arrived and offered to enter the forest. He went in, alone, with only his dog for company. The dog came to a pond, but an arm came out of the water and dragged the dog under. The hunter fetched help and slowly bucketed out the pond, until he found a wild man lying at the bottom—covered in hair with skin the color of rusty iron. The hunter tied up the wild man and carried him off to the castle, where the King locked him in an iron cage in the courtyard, and gave the key into the keeping of the Queen.

One day the King's eight-year-son dropped his golden ball into the wild man's cage. He asked the man to give it back.

Iron John answered, "Not until you have opened the cage door."

For two days the boy said, "No." On the third day he said, "I can't open the door because I don't know where the key is."

The wild man replied, "It's under your mother's pillow."

The boy stole the key and opened the cage, pinching and wounding his finger as he did so. Afraid, he cried out, "Wild man, don't go away, or I'll get a beating!"

The wild man turned around, picked up the boy, put him on his shoulders and strode off into the forest . . .

Robert had played a drum throughout; whether it was the insistent beat, his delivery, or our increasing commitment to follow whatever happened, I do not know, but it had been compelling. I

53

looked around to notice other men leaning forward, like little boys urging a friendly uncle to carry on. But he would not be swayed yet.

We would look at the story from three different viewpoints. The rational level took the characters to represent outer figures in the world, where King and Queen could be seen as father and mother. The psychological level saw the characters as representing inner figures in the psyche; the Hunter as an inner brave part of us, the Wild Man as our potential spontaneity. The mythological level saw characters and events as representing universal energies, forces in the world. So the golden ball might be a child's abundant joy in life, inevitably lost as it grows up, and the Wild Man a force in nature that can never be completely contained by human effort. We moved back and forth between these levels, using the tale as a landscape into which we each had our own entry point.

I went over my impressions: suspicion of the forest, admiration and jealousy of the hunter, fear of the wild man. If I had to pick my place in this story it was at the pond in the forest—the dog had been pulled down but no help was yet at hand. But at least I had got into the forest. My intention from the last workshop had brought me here to seek an unknown force. This figure in the pond was close, an ancient, natural, deep-rooted masculine power. I could not see him, but I yearned to. I wanted to be the boy going off on his shoulders to some unknown adventure in the forest. I wanted to have some of his wild energy for myself.

In ancient societies there were clear guidelines on how to wake such powerful beings inside a male. But this was done at a proper time and in a proper place, usually at the third stage of the boy's development and only when he was ready. Before this would come "Bonding with the Mother and Separation from the Mother" which took place from nought to seven years old and covered essential nurturing. Then came "Bonding with the Father and Separation from the Father," generally from seven to fourteen, when the son would spend time with the father, watching him work, play, and relate to other men. The third stage was this "Appearance of the

Male Mother," the wild man in the story, an unrelated older male who would initiate the boy into manhood.

As I heard this, something inside me winced. I knew I had not completed any of these stages, no wonder I still felt like a boy. But then, as other men spoke, I realized that I was not an isolated case. Not only did every man in this room have a tale of how he had missed these rites of passage, but Robert Bly assured us that the rites had not been active in society for a very long time. This absence, he contended, was at least partly responsible for the present confusion.

Although the bonding with the mother may happen nowadays, the separation rarely does. This leaves the son stuck in the mother's force field for too long, unable or unwilling to steal the key to the wild man's cage, which is under her pillow—"Just where Freud said it would be. . . ." The increasing number of single mothers bringing up sons will not help. A boy requires a male to "show him how to be a man." Without a same-sex role model something will be missing. Women who have been wounded by abusive men may teach the son that all men are abusive. So the boy grows up distrusting his male identity and other men. But we must not blame the mother; it is not her job to send the boy away, it is the responsibility of the father (and other older men) to come and fetch him.

But the father is, typically, too busy—so caught up in work that he can ill afford to recognize the son's need. The German psychologist Alexander Mitscherlich (in his book *Society Without the Father*) suggests that the absence of the father is one result of the industrial revolution, when men left the fields and were put to work in distant factories, away from their homes. Sons were unable to see the father at work. He would leave early and return late, often tired and irritable, drained of useful paternal energy. There was no time for the bonding to happen.

This creates a hole inside the son which he may fill with one of two unhappy choices—rejection or blind acceptance. The boy may resent the work that takes the father away, distrust the absent father, and turn in an opposite direction. Or he may worship from afar the demanding god that takes Dad away, bury his feelings of abandonment, and yearn to follow the absent father's footsteps.

I had vacillated between these two extremes, alternately embracing and rejecting theatre without really knowing why. My father's work kept him away and I grew up believing that work in general, theatre specifically must be more important than family in general, me specifically. When I follow this maxim, my own family feel abandoned; when I reject it, I sit around blaming Dad, theatre, and Shakespeare—anyone will do—for an imperfect childhood.

But even if he had chosen to be around more, traditionally the father would not be responsible for moving his son out towards the world of work. It was the job of the mentor, the initiator, to take the boy away from the family altogether and guide him in a suitable direction. This figure is also generally missing in our culture.

There are few responsible older men capable of inspiring younger men to follow them out into the world. And even fewer aware of this essential task. This is not surprising as men who have lost their own inspiration do not know what to pass on. The essence of male initiation was that it led the youth to something beyond himself, to a meaning inherent in the tribe, in the community, in the world itself. But meaning, for many modern men over the last century, has been firmly rooted in materialism. The old equation "He's a good man—he believes in God" changed to "He's good—he makes a lot of money." The current malaise may be a symptom telling us that this is no longer enough. As Alvin Toffler points out in *Eco-Spasm:*

> Indeed, what we are seeing today is not simply an economic upheaval, but something far deeper, something that cannot be understood within the framework of conventional economics. This is why increasingly mystified economists complain that 'The old rules don't work any longer.' What is happening, no

more, no less, is the breakdown of industrial civilization on the planet . . . Those who [deny this] . . . forget that economic breakdown may be a symptom of a larger transformation and may be generated by forces that economists never think to study . . .

(p.3)

We have reached a cultural crossroads; propelled here by old, worn out beliefs but nervous about looking for new ones. If faith in the old God was epitomized in the *Book of Job*, faith in the material god may well be challenged by the growing list of jobless. The belief that "progress" is always good whatever the cost, can be seen to be fallible, now that we have a clearer idea of what the cost actually is. Now we know that the more we produce the more waste we create, and the more we progress the fewer people we need to do the work. But while our noble leaders continue to believe in the fantasy of "eternal growth," more people lose faith in the system. Without a living myth to believe in, there is little for men to teach boys except confusion and emptiness.

So what was this mysterious process called Initiation which we kept circling around and seemed to be the central point of all our discussions? We were invited to participate with our imaginations first, as we headed back into the Story:

When the wild man reached the dark forest he put the boy down and said, "You will not see your father and mother again; but you may stay with me, if you do as I say. I have gold and other treasure, more than anyone else in the world."

In the morning he took the boy to a spring and said, "I want you to make sure nothing falls into this golden spring while I am gone."

The boy sat there: sometimes he saw a golden fish, or a golden snake in the water. Then his wounded finger began hurting; without thinking, he dipped it in the water. It instantly turned gold. Iron John came back and scolded him.

The second day the boy rubbed his hurting finger through his hair; a single hair fell into the spring and turned gold. The wild man gave him a last warning.

On the third day the boy sat, determined not to move his painful finger, and began to look at his reflection in the water. He leant down to look right into his own eyes, but his long hair fell in and turned gold. He covered his head with a handkerchief, but Iron John knew what had happened and said, "You have failed the test and can no longer remain here. Go out into the world and learn about poverty. But if you are ever in trouble come to the edge of the forest and call "Iron John" three times. I will help you."

Hiding his gold hair under a hat, the youth walked for a long time until he came to a distant castle. There he worked in the kitchen and swept the ashes. One day he was told to serve the King, but refused to remove his hat in the King's presence. The cook was told to fire the boy but swapped him for the gardener's boy.

Once, on a hot day, while working alone in the garden he took his head covering off but the sun reflected on his golden hair and glittered through the window of the Princess. She went to the window, caught sight of the boy and ordered him to bring her flowers. He put his hat on and took her a bunch of wild flowers, but she pulled his hat off. He tried to run away but she thrust some gold coins into his hand. He left her room and gave the coins to the gardener for his children to play with. The next two days the same thing happened, except he held onto his hat. The Princess couldn't get his hat off, and he gave away the coins she gave him . . .

I had been saddened and worried that the boy would never see his parents again. It made his choice to go with the wild man so final, so irrevocable. One man asked why the father could not go off with the boy as well. Robert Bly answered him with a statement that froze me, "A boy cannot become a man until the day his father dies . . ." My mind was wiped clean of other thoughts. In a moment of peculiar clarity I saw how my numbness related to this statement and that the underlying drive was to achieve manhood in the wake of this death. Even the awful elation at hearing the news became clearer, less guilt-ridden, if my father's life had stood in the way of this task.

As I tried to think why this was, images rose up to fill my mind. An invisible but potent umbilical cord, representing the energies that bind son to father, threatening to keep him forever a boy in the father's presence. The initial, immense disparity in size—one minuscule sperm generated by a towering Giant. The deep thundering voice felt as a fetus and heard as a child. (And I had Richard the bloody Third tell me to "siddown and shadup.") The godlike power of this stranger with his magical hold over mother. The boy's weakness hopelessly pitted against the Giant's strength through childhood . . .

In my case fame had reinforced this Giant image. As I entered my teens, needing to see my father as a normal (and therefore limited) human being from whom it was advisable to move away, others confirmed what a great Giant he was. For this and doubtless many other reasons, the invisible ties had never been cut. I had relied on the Giant to support me way beyond the time it was appropriate for him to do so. Now he was dead, I was lost. I felt the depressing weight of all this and simultaneously a stirring deep in my bones. A faint excitement, as if help was at hand, as if there did exist some possibility of recovery.

For it was exactly such filial dependence that traditional initiation would sever. In which case the death of the father would not be physical but metaphorical. Indeed, the real death is of the boy's own image of himself as a boy. As the anthropologist Mircea Eliade has written:

> The term initiation in the most general sense denotes a body of rites and oral teachings whose purpose is to produce a decisive alteration in the religious and social status of the person to be

initiated. In philosophical terms, initiation is equivalent to a basic change in existential condition; the novice emerges from his
ordeal endowed with a totally different being from that which
he possessed before his initiation; he has become *another* . . .

(*Rites and Symbols of Initiation*, p. x)

This is why, as in "Iron John," the boy "will not see his parents
again." Not because he will never again set eyes on the human
beings who gave him birth, but because after his initiation they
will no longer exert the parental influence that they did before. He
will never see them as parents in the same way again. Before this
can happen he must undergo separation and endure many ordeals.

Separation physically removes the boy from his parents. He is
taken off to live in a secluded area, with only fellow initiates and
male elders for company. Emotionally he can no longer be dependent on the parents, or unduly influenced by them. It is in this type
of setting that a boy may first become aware that part of him is
golden. In the story gold appears in the wounded finger, suggesting that where we are wounded, there may also lie some golden
potential. This gold spreads into one hair, and then after "looking
into his own eyes," over the whole head of hair. The time alone
gives the boy a sense of his self worth, as an individual, not as a
son. It is necessary that a boy feels "golden" before he embarks on
his ordeals, otherwise he may doubt his ability to survive them, or
worse, give up.

Now the youth must endure a series of trials, interspersed with
learning dances, poems, songs, tribal secrets, and myths. The elders
impart the cultural history of the tribe, and the importance of the
individual parents is lessened. Like a variation on the parental marriage cliché, "You're not losing a son, you're gaining a daughter . . .",
in effective initiation boys don't lose a personal father but gain a
cultural one, supported by mentors. The father is no longer the sole
occupant of the son's male psyche. As different men earn a place of
honor there, the father is naturally reduced from godlike size. As the

father is shown to be part of the larger culture like all the other men, he becomes, like them, a human being.

In the story the youth works in the kitchen under a cook. He rakes ashes, which could mean raking the ashes of his past, clearing the burnt-out dreams that threaten to stop the cooking of future food. He visits the King but does not please him yet. There is more work to be done. He moves into the garden, working under a gardener, learning about earth, nurturing nature, and creating beauty. He attracts the attention of the Princess, but does not yet wish to stay with her. It was important that he did not show off the gold he had already earned, but hid it while he carried on learning, passing more trials:

> Not long after this, a war broke out. The King's troops were outnumbered so the youth asked to be allowed to fight. The others laughed and showed him to a horse which was lame in one foot. He rode it to the forest and called "Iron John" three times. He asked for a war horse but was also given a great band of warriors, all clad in iron. He galloped into battle, saved the King from defeat and pursued the enemy to the last man. Then he returned to the forest and asked for his lame horse back. He went back to the castle and was laughed at when he said he had helped in the battle.

> The King and the Princess were curious about the strange knight and arranged a festival at which the Princess would throw a golden apple on each of three days. Each day the youth acquired a horse and armor from Iron John—first red, then white, then black—rode to the festival, caught the apple and galloped off. On the third day the King's men chased him and wounded him in the leg, his horse reared up, his helmet fell off and everyone saw his golden hair.

> The next day the Princess asked the gardener about his boy. The gardener said, "What a strange boy! He's been showing my children three golden apples he has won." The King summoned the youth, and the Princess pulled off his hat, revealing his

golden hair. He showed the King the apples and admitted his true part in the battle. The King offered him a reward of his choice. The youth asked for the Princess' hand in marriage. She went over and kissed him.

His mother and father came to the wedding and were overjoyed as they had given up hope of seeing him again. During the wedding banquet a baronial lord entered with a great retinue. He walked up to the youth and embraced him. Then he said, "I am Iron John. I was under a spell that made me a wild man, but you have released me from it. All the treasures that I possess shall be yours.

I had been shocked that the youth had wiped out the opposing army "to the last man." But there may well be forces inside us that keep sabotaging our best intentions, or forces outside who would limit our freedom. These may not accept a cease-fire or peace treaty, and need to be destroyed. As men we may need to access this capacity. But it must be done with discrimination. The story suggests that this is gained by contact with the feminine. It is after his time in the garden, and after meeting the Princess, that he goes into battle. If he had not been prepared to fight the kingdom would have been invaded. If he had simply gone on tending the garden he would have ended up without bride or treasure. Flower power doesn't always work.

Other men, too, were nervous of the wild man, thinking him a proponent of violent male aggression. It became necessary to distinguish between "wild" and "savage." In the story the wild man is never violent; he lends the youth fierceness (horse, armor, weapons, and armed men) but only to defend the realm. And it is this same wild man who is actually a baronial Lord, with treasure to pass to the youth.

An image of a three-layered man passed in front of my eyes, like a computer graphic. I could see the outer surface which was masculine, then an inner layer which was feminine, but underneath this was a deep masculine core. If the first layer was physical masculine identity, then the second layer possessed softer, caring, emotional qualities; but it was the third man that held the real key. This was the realm of the Wild Man; a deep underlying structure of essential male energy.

The graphic in my mind's eye began to move, and energy passed between the layers. It became apparent that the second layer was a filtering system; the deep male energy would pass through the nurturing feminine layer and could be used with sensitive discrimination by the surface man.

But if the second layer was inactive then the wild energy moved straight into the surface man, causing a "male overload," leading to the indiscriminate violence typical of the macho bully, and the abusive Patriarch.

But if, on the other hand, the third layer was inactive, then the surface man is filled with sensitivity but has no strong foundation to support him.

So if some men have exchanged access to the tougher third layer for access to the caring second layer, they would still be imbalanced, just in a different way. A new balance will only be found if all three layers are active.

Somehow I made myself a victim of this imbalance, and now, when a deeper strength was needed, instead of gaining access to the third layer I had shut off the second as well. I was uncomfortably aware of a physical hunger in my body for this third man.

But all this initiation business came from ancient rituals and an alien culture. It would be naive to think a modern man could be helped by acting out old tribal rites. Robert Bly suggested that we could use the coded tales of initiation, hidden in mythology and fairy tales, filter them through new psychological understanding and see what might be relevant to us.

I went back to "my" place in the story, standing by the stagnant pond in the forest. The dog had been pulled down as if some animal instinct in me had been pulled into the pond, but for some reason I did not want to fetch help. Why was I scared of what I would find there?

This place in the tale was prior to the discovery of the wild man, so it was possible that the fear came from ignorance. Maybe I had never seen a wild man, caged in a courtyard, as a boy. Perhaps my father had not brought his spontaneous, natural side into our home.

And then I remembered two stories he had told me. Once, when playing Richard III on a long post-war tour of Germany, he had arrived at a new theatre feeling completely shattered. He was certain he did not have the energy to go on stage that night. The Tannoy system was turned on and he had heard the audience, gathering, muttering, expectant. He found himself filling up with energy, he went on stage and gave a blazing performance, "The best of my life." When it ended he could not remember anything about it, was frightened by the experience, and drank himself to sleep. Years later he feared that Vivien Leigh would go mad while playing Blanche Dubois in *A Streetcar Named Desire*. He said she let the part take her over completely and blamed this possession for her future mental instability.

It struck me that he had found good reason to fear such wild energy, and that he had determined to keep it out of his home. He had utilized it under strict control, but only in the theatre. He had never "emptied out the pond" and looked at the creature who supplied it.

So it would be a stranger to me, unknown and unseen. I felt I was chasing shadows; every time I thought I could touch something tangible it dissolved or faded from view.

When the practical advice came, I did not want to hear it. According to Robert Bly the stagnant pond is a kind of numbness. The only way to get beneath the surface of this pond was to work through our area of greatest numbness. There we will find the deepest hurt. For hurt feelings can act as the opposite of feelings; where our feelings were hurt in childhood is where we will try not to feel anything in adulthood.

I recoiled from this statement, my back forced against my chair as if to break it. I knew my numbness was connected to my father and to his death. And I didn't want to know. Even though part of me recognized Rainer Maria Rilke's poetic insight:

Sometimes a man stands up during supper and walks outdoors, and keeps on walking, because of a church that stands somewhere in the East.

And his children say blessings on him as if he were dead.

And another man, who remains inside his own house, stays there, inside the dishes and in the glasses, so that his children have to go far out into the world toward that same church, which he forgot.

(from the *Selected Poems of Rainer Maria Rilke*, translated by Robert Bly)

An instinct was calling me to dive into the pond, but I was scared of drowning. This poem seemed to say I must seek out an old haunted church, enter the graveyard at night, dig up a few graves, and play with the bones. Frankly, the idea scared me shitless. Having recently finished with the memorial, I wanted to leave my father behind, get out of his shadow, and get on with my life. Surely there must be a way to reach the Third Man without going via my father?

My determination shifted subtly away from this kind of exploration. Without realizing it I withdrew my trust and hid behind the battlements. If I didn't trust the advice it couldn't be right, could it?

As the day wound up Robert Bly suggested that those interested in men's work get together in small groups and meet regularly. My defensive hackles rose some more. I looked around and took refuge in arrogance. I wasn't going to meet with any of these poor wounded people and talk about my stuff. I did feel a tiny twinge of guilt as the generous energy shriveled. But whatever had been born in this room would not survive outside it, yet. Years of training—and a few beers—soon hushed the tiny voice that demanded action. It would have to wait. What the hell, it was used to it.

CHAPTER FOUR

The Show Must Go On

Throughout the next year I strove to ignore the call to adventure, and found instead a sense of purpose in work. But I was treading water in a swelling sea—kicking ever harder to keep my head above the surface. Deep down, the Third Man knew I was doing the wrong thing, and was not going to let me get away with it. Or, as Snoopy once said, "He who lives by the sneaky backhand cross court drop shot . . . dies by the sneaky backhand cross court drop shot." The only thing able to penetrate the defense of successful work was failure.

Joseph Campbell, in *The Hero With a Thousand Faces,* warns of the consequences that await he who refuses such a call to adventure:

> Even though he returns for a while to his familiar occupations, they may be found unfruitful. A series of signs of increasing force will then become visible until . . . the summons can no longer be denied.
>
> (*p.*56)

And for the next few months I plunged into "familiar occupation" with a vengeance. I was in pre-production for a new thriller, *Abracadaver,* and the Los Angeles production of a new play, *Meetin's on the Porch.* I was recasting both the West End and touring productions of *Shirley Valentine,* and planning *Time and the Conways,* in which I would direct my mother and both my sisters.

The "signs" were shrugged off at the time as technical hitches. The rewrite of *Abracadaver* was late, which meant the leading actor, Frank Langela, and I had to sign contracts without a final script. Rehearsal dates for *Meetin's on the Porch* kept being postponed until they clashed with the second tour of *Shirley.* I ended up directing the first two weeks of rehearsals in Los Angeles, then handing over the reins to the playwright, Donald MacKechnie, while I returned to England. Once back I rehearsed *Shirley* in the mornings while auditioning for *Abracadaver* in the afternoons. It required clinical organization to avert the threatened chaos. But if I had needed to be busy in order to deny the summons, I had succeeded.

Abracadaver was gearing up to be a big production. An American star, expensive design, composer, musicians, the works. Frank Langela arrived from New York, full of disarming charm. At our first meeting he insisted that he liked to work closely with directors, and he wanted us to support each other fully. I was impressed. He was a tall, powerful looking man, at ease with his Broadway star status, replete with animal magnetism and sexual energy. We started nightly meetings with the writers to finalize the script, and scoured the West End for prospective cast members. I was so keen to appear the efficient director I hardly mentioned the situation at home.

Meanwhile our second child was past its due date. Shelley was beginning to worry but was determined not to show it. I was actually determined not to see it and remained unavailable. I was in one of those strange sado-masochistic British (or is it just male?) moods, where I secretly enjoyed the pain I felt and caused. In a funny way it made me feel strong. I was wearing the male protective cloak of "duty." Like the "Emperor's New Clothes," as long as I believed in this cloak, it would keep me covered, at least in my own imagination.

Our daughter, Ali, was born on February 13, at seven a.m., the morning after the first day of rehearsal for *Abracadaver*. She was born at home, into the safe hands of Dr. Michel Odent, while I stood holding Shelley upright in a birthing pool. Michel had called the night before, saying he would be in our area and thought he might as well spend the night. When Shelley went into labor three hours after he arrived, I scarcely had time to marvel at his powers of intuition. Maybe he knew my wife simply needed someone around who would not piss off at the first reasonable opportunity, in order to relax enough to give birth. As it turned out I was particularly pleased with myself for ending up a mere fifteen minutes late for the second day of rehearsal. What's more, there was something conscious about it; a peculiar urge to prove to the cast that what had happened was worth being a little late for, but not too much. A sort of fashionable new-man tardiness. Certainly not enough for them to question my commitment to the show. Shelley later told me she knew she would have to deliver before rehearsals started if she wanted me there.

Over the following weeks I moved between the new baby at home and the new play at work in a daze. I was caught between two worlds, both demanding total dedication, and aware I could not meet these demands. As I entered each reality, the one left behind became unreal, dreamlike. But there was a crucial difference. When I walked into rehearsal, homelife was instantly shut off, terrifyingly unimportant, a forgotten dream. While when I went home, the play and its problems stayed with me, like a nightmare that keeps surging to the forefront of consciousness, holding the new baby, but listening for the phone to ring.

At home Shelley was probably more supportive towards me than I was to her, at work the support was more than I had bargained for. I was working with a Broadway star who was used to an active role in all areas of production. I had an unofficial co-director on board. Things should have come to a head at the end of the second week when, still without a final script, we did some improvisation. In one such exercise Frank invented a clever, but cruel, play on words, which the actress in the scene found difficult to accept, since her character was trying to be helpful. Frank informed her that he had script approval, and would say what he wanted to. I called a break and tried to reason with him. When all else failed I reminded him of our agreement to support each other which he answered straightforwardly enough: "Yes. That means you support me."

The challenge of "whose production is it anyway?" had been laid down. But I could not pick up the gauntlet. I was nervous enough of the conflict it would cause, but terrified of losing. Having willingly put all my eggs into the career basket, I had too much at stake to risk an early departure due to "creative differences." Behind the personal defeat, public humiliation loomed in my mind. What about the family name? What will people think?

I had thought that success would give me strength, and conveniently forgot that I would need strength to earn success. There was no band of warriors waiting to come out of the forest and fight. There was no route through to the Third Man. Now, head to head with a strong man, something inside had wilted. I stood down from the challenge—and got fired later.

I went to the actress and privately promised her that the line would be cut. I conspired with the writers. When they later said this line made the leading character deeply unsympathetic, it was duly cut. I held up a white flag on the surface, while fighting an underground, rearguard action against unconditional surrender. But these small devious victories would not win the war.

The technical rehearsal proved a nightmare, complete with potentially dangerous magic equipment and sliding set pieces which didn't slide. We opened three days late, still without a mutually agreed upon script, and heading for trouble. We were not ready for our scheduled transfer into the West End, and held a crisis meeting. Everyone had changes to suggest—new music, new actors, new co-writers, a co-director to choreograph Vegas-style production numbers—but no one could agree which to pursue. In the face of this stalemate it was finally decided to cancel the transfer, wait for the dust to settle, and work some new ideas into another try-out. So far so clear.

One evening the next week I arrived at the theatre early. I went into Frank's dressing room to find him talking to a man I didn't know. Both looked startled, but Frank recovered first and introduced me to the man mentioned at the meeting as a possible co-director.

It was a moment of suspended time. My heart took a slow elevator ride to the pit of my stomach, while my ears burned. I knew what this meeting meant. But I refused to admit it. I fell back on expensive nice boy training. I extended a hand, heard the words "Hello, nice to meet you" emerge, as if without effort, from my mouth, shook the conspirator's hand and turned to Frank. I thought, "Et tu, Frankie?" but said, "Have a good show . . . I'll see you later," and retired with—I like to think—some grace.

I walked out of the theatre in the grip of an adrenaline surge, chest pounding like a rap beat in a passing car, vision swirling as I strove for equilibrium. A few deep breaths and a couple of drinks later . . . and I had convinced myself that the dressing room cabal was about Vegas-style production numbers. Someone had just forgotten to tell me.

Frank later apologized for the surprise; nothing had been decided, everything was still up in the air, just discussing possibilities. I hadn't the courage to ask if one of these was replacing me. And so the torture dragged on for weeks. Possibilities became probabilities, probabilities became a new production. The new production became a new supporting cast, a new script, and a new director.

The final news came over a last lunch with Frank. I couldn't blame him. I would probably have done the same thing in his shoes. Nor could I get angry. I limply wished him luck and went away feeling about two feet tall, five years old, and sick.

I ran away to Spain, as I thought then, to lick my wounds. As it turned out I spent a couple of weeks avoiding them. Had I been possessed of the natural ability to lick wounds, it may not have been necessary to write about them. But there we go.

It was the first time for long while that I had the opportunity to be with Shelley, the first ever to welcome Ali into the world, and to reassure Troy he had not been abandoned as a result. But a previous program was still running. Somehow I couldn't stop it and start another. Inactivity would have been too threatening, introspection too dangerous. I couldn't quite relax. When I went to the beach to play with my son, I could concentrate on our game for about ten minutes before my mind, seemingly of its own accord, would turn itself to future work. Here was a young human soul, offering me his golden ball, wanting me to share his magical world. And I turned him down, preferring to head indoors on a sunny day, swapping golden sand for a parched script, time with my son for *Time and the Conways*. I returned to England a week earlier than my family to rehearse the second West End takeover of *Shirley Valentine*. Two days later I opened the *Daily Mail* and saw, splashed across the gossip page, the large headline, "The Murder Victim is an Olivier." It took me several attempts to read the whole article, which was, indeed, about *Abracadaver*. I felt like a voodoo doll on a bad day, stuck full of needles that effortlessly punctured the defenseless surface with burning accuracy. I couldn't create any distance between me and the production. It was not the play that had failed, but me. And now it was public knowledge. Even in failure I was denied a personal identity. "*An* Olivier." My first name was irrelevant, the actual person of no value except as gossip fodder.

The panic button had been well and truly pushed. I started pacing aimlessly around the house while my body called on old medicine. The heat of humiliation was gradually replaced by numbing ice, a drip feed from the brain to the heart. By the time I left the house the pain had been anaesthetized, leaving only paranoia. On the way to rehearsal, I knew every sod on the tube had read the article, and every look was filled with damning knowledge.

That afternoon Willy Russell and the producer, Bill Kenwright, joined the rehearsal. During a tea break Bill was laughing about a bad review his latest production had received. I muttered something about "not having had a very good review myself today." Bill shrugged it off saying, "It's all rubbish isn't it?" and turned back to our latest *Shirley.* To him it was water off a duck's back, to me it was ingested poison. Was it simply the difference between a self-made man and the son of a famous man? I wasn't sure, all I knew was that his defenses were adequate, mine were not.

I went home, fed up and looking for inspiration. I avoided the TV and flicked through some old books until I found something to match my mood.

> Often in actual life, and not infrequently in the myths and popular tales, we encounter the dull case of the call unanswered; for it is always possible to turn the ear to other interests. Refusal of the summons converts the adventure into its negative. *Walled in boredom, hard work, or "culture," the subject loses the power of significant affirmative action and becomes a victim to be saved.* His flowering world becomes a wasteland of dry stones and his life feels meaningless . . . Whatever house he builds, it will be a house of death . . . All he can do is create new problems for himself and await the gradual approach of his disintegration.
> (*Hero with a Thousand Faces,* p.59, my emphasis)

Charming. Even the *Daily Mail* had figured out I was a "victim." But the events of this day were to prove a turning point. I had a week to be by myself, to experience a little of this wasteland. Gradually, however reluctantly, my mind began to shift, allowing thoughts of my father in for the first time since the men's workshop. I went back over the notes I had taken that weekend and was struck by one that read, "Even though your parents may be dead, that's no reason not to communicate with them—some people are easier to talk to when they're dead."

My father's birthday was approaching. I picked up my pen and started writing.

MELTING THE STONE

ON THE EVE OF YOUR EIGHTY-THIRD BIRTHDAY

I loved you—not as most sons love their fathers,
Rugged mountains to be climbed in awe-filled trepidation, But
as the stripling who sees the Great Oak wither and fall.

So unkind, not having a private Hero for a dad,
But a man with a Name, a Face,
That others wanted to possess.

I could only watch the shadows,
As they swarmed around you, obscuring the light,
As you lost your battle with mortality.

Leaving anger not acceptance, profanity not prayer.
Though with a wish for both;
A longing for God and a need for applause . . .

I felt I had scraped the surface of something, maybe that mythic pond, dipped a toe in to test the temperature. It felt very cold and very deep. A mite too dangerous to approach alone. But on the other hand, there was no one I could trust to come with me. It was an apparent stalemate. But I made occasional attempts to free myself.

One such attempt led Shelley and me to a lecture given by an Indian meditation teacher, Maharaji. This chubby, happy man draped in a designer suit had his own unique brand of cross-cultural slang: "Remember, even if you win the rat race—you are still a rat!" I listened with interest to his advice to "Look at your life and examine the *big* moments that killed the trust, innocence, and joy of the child," but I was totally resistant to the ensuing soft sell. Interested parties should sign up for training sessions in his methods . . .

Soon after this I had dinner with an elderly Irish writer friend, Michael Sayers. When I finished talking about recent events, he

looked at me across the table intently, "I can only say this as a negative . . . don't get a teacher." He had many years' experience of
groups involved in esoteric study, and believed most teachers were
ultimately selfish and destructive. Many people in cultish groups
become dependent on the person in charge, who may also have a
vested and/or financial interest in keeping the others attached.

I had narrowly avoided this kind of relationship a few years
before. While researching a group of twelfth-century heretics, the
Cathars, I was introduced to a modern group in Glendale, Califor-
nia who shared very similar beliefs. Captivated by the subject, I
soon became intrigued by these "Niscenes," and their leader, a self-
styled priest called Jonathan Murro.

The Niscenes claimed to follow the Cathars' belief in freedom
from religious tyranny. It was only when I saw how imprisoned
these people were by strict adherence to the ideas of Mr. Murro
that I pulled away and left them to it. There were elderly members
who had followed instructions for thirty-odd years, yet were still
urged to attend every meeting and lecture. Hadn't they learnt yet?
I could see now that these eternal students had sacrificed independence for security. In fact, they had never really broken away from
their parents, only transferred their wish for Godlike parental protection onto a teacher.

As the dinner discussion continued we made an important dis-
tinction between a teacher (or guru) and an advisor (or mentor). In
terms of the initiatory process, both could help the pupil achieve
the first goal of separation from the parents, and both would su-
pervise some trials to make a change in his condition. The crucial
difference would not appear until later. What should be the return
of the initiate to the world he left would be encouraged by the
mentor but discouraged by the guru.

I understood this through an image of an invisible, or psychic,
umbilical cord. During an intense learning process a student's cord
will be separated from its previous natural attachment to his parents. The initiator holds this cord himself, becoming the nurturing
"male mother." But at the end of a certain period the cord is cut,

and the initiate is reborn an independent man, with responsibilities in the larger community.

The danger with a guru is that he will never cut the cord and so denies his students their independence. Instead of returning them to the larger community, he tugs on the cord and offers a replacement community, smaller, safer, and under his control. Here the student can stay in a state of constant initiation, always learning but forever dependent.

It may be difficult to distinguish the mentor from the guru until it is too late, until the bait has been swallowed and the pupil hooked. I left that evening understanding a little more about my reluctance to rely on others, particularly since my experience with Jonathan Murro. And I was determined not to trust anyone until I knew they would let me go.

However, even as I avoided dependence in one area, I slipped towards it in another; directing a play starring my mother and two sisters. I wasn't exactly making bold moves away from family influence.

At the time it had been decided upon, I was confident of having two shows in the West End, and having been seen to earn my spurs. As it was, *Shirley* was still afloat but *Abracadaver* had sunk without trace—the news that the second production had swiftly followed mine to an early grave provided me with my largest whoop of *schadenfreude* in a long time. But the experience had left me vulnerable to accusations of "family affairs," half suspecting that I was allowing my mother to rebirth me, having recently died as the "murder victim."

In the event *Time and the Conways* proved an immensely valuable experience; not least because one particular performance would plant seeds of insight to await future harvest.

The morning after we opened at Theatre Clwyd in North Wales, a doctor rang to say that Joan had chronic bronchitis and couldn't perform that night. There were no understudies and no means of informing the audience of a cancellation. When it became clear that no other actress could be found in time to read my mother's part, I agreed to do it. And so, interrupted only by a very short argument about wearing her wig, I prepared for my one and only performance on the professional stage—as Mrs. Conway.

I calmly rehearsed with a bemused cast in the afternoon. It was only as I heard the half-hour call over the Tannoy system that my nerves started to jangle. There was no reason to worry, I would have the text in my hand, all I had to do was read. But something about the situation called up a peculiar dread. As if I was doing something that I should not be doing.

I walked on stage, literally in mother's footsteps, feeling totally exposed. An instant of pure fear; my eyes refused to focus on the words. But then the adrenaline kicked through, and I began. Having lived outside the play for so long, it was extraordinary suddenly to be part of its life. I was in a strange world, like a painter transported into a landscape of his own creation. I managed to negotiate my way through it without getting lost, and, afterwards, through a good deal of the promised bottle of Scotch without falling down.

These weird sensations were to be grounded in reality by two upcoming events: a residential men's weekend with Robert Bly and, prior to that, a London Convivium lecture with James Hillman.

By now I had figured out that archetypal psychology was about injecting imagination into old-style psychological thinking. It took images to be important in themselves, not just meat for further interpretations. James Hillman was the leading voice in this field, and his subject this evening was "The Ethics of Showbusiness."

I sat down expecting to be vindicated in my distrust of acting, to be reassured that it was dangerous to spend a large pert of your life pretending to be someone else. But it wasn't to be.

His basic premise was that we are now living in a world so full of the media that the ethics of showbusiness have become the ethics of life. The world is increasingly defined in media terms and seen through media images. This has led to a certain inflated self regard.

MELTING THE STONE

There is an increasing tendancy for "media coverage" to be an item on the national news. Journalistic comment on how an event is covered can be as extensive as comment about the event itself. Recent stories about the royal family bear this out. Broadsheets which affect to despise tasteless gossip can still slip it onto the front page disguised as a news story about what those awful tabloids are doing. On TV one night I saw a new review show featuring *Entertainment Tonight*. Here was a program which was reviewing a program which was about the making of yet other programs. The mirrors seemed endless.

But as we move inside the hall of mirrors we find a different set of rules apply. In this media world morality is changed. "Good" and "bad" are no longer intrinsic virtues belonging to a thing or person, but are used to describe performance. "Was he good?" means "Did he give a good performance?" not "Is he a good person?" In recent American history, Oliver North's performance as the all-American patriotic hero during the Irangate scandal was so impressive that he was made a hero and forgiven for his confessed crimes.

Metaphors from showbiz are used in all areas of life. Self-improvement is called "getting your act together." As we vote more performers into office, so media-speak move into politics; when politicians "come across well" it is the performance not the message we mean. When Ronald Reagan was asked how he felt about being upstaged by Gorbachev (would Roosevelt have been asked such a question about Stalin?) he replied, "I worked with Errol Flynn, you know." The movie set provides the example that gives the political event validity. Life imitates Showbiz.

Some of the ten or more principles Hillman named in his talk were:

1) *The Work Ethic*
   Productivity is paramount—everything is sacrificed to The Work. The primary commitment is to the job, not to a person, team, or set of beliefs.

2) *The Show Must Go On*

Endurance is essential. Personal feelings are sacrificed for
The Show; interior needs are willingly set aside in the complete dedication of self to public. The interior person is ap-
propriated by the external world.

3) *Stay in Character*

You are not two people—one in public another in private—
only one, the public one. One is one's appearance because
one's appearance is one's work (i.e. one's work is to appear
. . .). The primary modern question is not about "who we
are" but about "what we do" because what we do *is* who
we are.

I had that sinking feeling in my stomach that told me I was
hearing something I needed to hear but did not want to take on
board. I had just heard my father's rule book read out. He had put
his work first; he had become other characters so brilliantly that he
did not know who he was, only what he did—act. And I wanted
that choice to be proved a terrible mistake. My stage-fright was
part of that wish. I did not want to act because I did not want my
father to act. He had sacrificed his identity, and I feared losing mine.

But I was blaming my father's loss of identity on acting, not on
work in general. Mainly because I was doing exactly the same as
he had done, and didn't want to see it. Except now I had. The past
year I had replicated his choice, putting work above family, plays
before children, imitation before life. I had tried to define myself
through work. A director first, a person second. A "human doing"
not a human being. Maybe it would have been fine if this activity,
the doing, had stemmed from a secure sense of being. But because
this activity was hiding a wound it could only ever be a temporary
bandage, not a permanent solution. It was time for a change of
tack, spurred on by the knowledge that this rule book had not,
finally, worked for my father. Nor could it work for me.

Hillman seemed to be encouraging the showbiz ethic trend, suggesting there may be a message hidden behind it, trying to call us

out from our private, hidden lives to a fuller engagement with the world. But I could only think of what this engagement had done to my father, and by extension to me.

I was very uneasy as the lecture finished, and used an invite to dinner with Noel Cobb, James Hillman, and others as an excuse to try and unload it. I didn't get very far. I described how my father had lived by this showbiz rule book, but he had not died happy. Hillman shifted his elegantly aging New England frame, and set his piercing, amused eyes on mine, "And what makes you think that we are supposed to be happy?" I was stopped short and lapsed into awkward silence. Questions whirled around my head: Why did I think he should have been happy?—Why did I believe that I should be happy? —Who did I know who was really happy, anyway?

I went home sulking. I had been made to look at a long-held dream. The wish to return to a fantasy childhood, where I could be eternally loved by happy parents. I saw the naiveté of this wish and was ashamed. What was this childish part of me that would not grow up? Why couldn't I get rid of it?

There were no answers to be found that night. And small comfort that I had started asking some of the right questions. The first real clue would be uncovered in an old, converted public school, in two weeks' time, two hundred miles away.

Chapter Five

The Stone Child

On a gloomy Friday afternoon in October I collected Jackie from his house and we drove to Dorset for the men's residential weekend conference, "Passion and Purpose in the Male Psyche." We were both more nervous than last year, though we did not admit it for a while. But the enforced jollity wore thin as the miles flashed by, dirty jokes giving way to uneasy silence. That underground room in Victoria seemed positively cozy now that we faced the prospect of two nights away from home, in an unknown setting full of unknown men. We bravely stopped at a pub on our final approach, before venturing into Gaunt's Rouse, the New Age conference center that was our destination.

We walked up to the registration table. My nerves were not soothed to learn the building was an ex-public school, and we would be sleeping in dorms. Maybe a little more fortification was in order. We asked when the bar would open. A certain amount of deeply mature panic set in on being told it was closed for the duration. This was the first of many habitual defenses to be undermined. We went upstairs and found a bedroom as far away as possible from signs of the other seventy men in various states of arrival. My heart sank further when our entry to the dining room heralded a seriously vegetarian meal. Did real New Age men *only* eat quiche? It was getting worse—no women, no booze, and no meat. What next?

We were ushered towards an elegant ballroom and instructed to sit on the chairs spread in semi-circles under the glistening chandeliers and ancestral portraits, facing a small, raised platform in front of a blazing log fire. I felt a bit better. Nothing too dangerous could happen in here, surely?

Robert Bly entered, looking more relaxed and colorful than at the previous men's event, perhaps because he wouldn't have to do all the work this time—or maybe he'd brought his own food. He introduced Michael Meade, an American drummer, storyteller, and mythologist of Irish descent who would be his cohort for the weekend. He was younger than Bly, and shorter—almost impish, in a tough New York street sort of way—with a pudding bowl of short black hair and a large Cuban drum.

They both looked around the room with mock concern, noting that in the States they worked in log cabins not ducal manors. They hoped the apparent sophistication of the setting would not prevent the commitment and honesty that this event would require. I had a nasty feeling that wherever we were going this weekend, it would be further and deeper than last year. This was quickly evidenced by Robert Bly's introduction.

He said that he was here because his father had been an alcoholic and because he had lived as a "failure" in his father's eyes for many years, writing unpublished poetry rather than working the family farm. Living with these burdens had encouraged him to look for positive sides to fathering, masculinity, and duty. These strange, remote meetings of men were, in part, a result of this soul searching. Here was a place where men could gather without the competition of sports and business, or the protective camaraderie of pubs and clubs. Here a different community feeling could develop, with different results:

When I am teaching with men, I am in that place again where something was broken with the father. And by staying there, some healing occurs.

Michael Meade's route towards this room was no less compelling. Growing up in a New York street gang in the fifties, he had learnt the value of stories the hard way. When faced by a rival gang and threatened with serious injury, the tales he spun had saved him. Drafted into the army for the Vietnam conflict, he had refused to follow senseless orders and was court-martialled. He spent a year in military prison, three months of which were in solitary confinement. He was eventually released after a hunger strike that left him weighing less than one hundred pounds. Later on he felt so distanced from the accepted way of the world he could not face leaving his house to walk down the street. Learning to drum was a way to communicate an older rhythm that held more connections for him. Mythology had given a context to the disparate pieces of his experience; working with men had given them a means of expression:

> Albert Camus said, 'A man's work is nothing more than to rediscover, through the detours of art, those one or two images in the presence of which his heart first opened.' If we open up the word art to include myth, emotion, and ritual, then modern men, through 'men's work,' are trying to rediscover the doorways to their hearts and the territories of the soul.
>
> (Michael Meade, *Men and the Water of Life*, p. 10)

Special conditions are required to create a "ritual space," where such doorways could be found and opened—a different place, committed intention, and responsible supervision. It would involve a separation from everyday life and a move into a self-contained area prepared for serious work. Some sacrifice or change of status is demanded on entry, after which the place is "sealed and heated." The participants stay inside but only for a limited time, and then return to normal life.

It sounded like a large, human pressure cooker. When I realized that our group had already met the first few conditions, I wondered if there was still time to leave. But then Michael Meade told us to clear the chairs away so we could perform an exercise to "seal and heat the space." Maybe the ballroom was not such a safe place to be after all.

We were to divide ourselves into two groups, those who wanted to go "up" this weekend, towards joy, and those who wanted to go "down" into grief. My anxiety finally defined itself as on the down-bound train.

We were about to play a tribal African warrior game. I quickly looked around and was slightly relieved to see most of the larger men on my side. Each group would take turns to sing an African chant while dancing wildly towards the opposition and signaling "traditional signs of respect," i.e. obscene gestures. The opposing side would retreat and work out their next gesture, ready to surge forward when the first side finished. Michael Meade pointed out an invisible line in the center which neither side was to cross, and sat on it, starting an insistent beat on his drum.

At first it seemed that there were not enough bodies to hide behind. No one wanted to be at the front of the advancing line, or come up with new gestures. Embarrassed smiles were flashed around, as if to excuse the diffident shuffling of feet as a necessary avoiding tactic. But gradually, as the rhythm began to sink in, a few men let go of inhibition, broke ranks, and urged the rest of us to greater effort. It went on and on, back and forth across the room, gaining energy all the time as more and more men abandoned their self-consciousness and threw themselves into the fray.

I felt as if I was being picked up by a large wave and gently wafted onto the waiting shore. Carried by a force larger than my-self, full of life, inspired by aggression and opposition, but not dangerous. The invisible line was a protective barrier, the surrounding tribe provided physical support and welcome anonymity. I found it too confronting to focus on a single face in the opposing group, but as long as I looked at them as a "them," I could maintain a strong voice and fierce posture.

By the final round the most reluctant among us had been moved to sweat and song. We finished with aplomb, broke into laughter, and then headed gratefully for our beds, barely aware of the invisible line we had crossed together.

The next morning we started working with the fairy story through whose images we would explore "Passion and Purpose in the Male Psyche." It was called "Prince Ivan and the Firebird," and would be told in sections, by Michael Meade, underlined and supported by masterful drumming:

In a certain kingdom, far away, there lived a mighty King. In the realm there was a young hunter, and the hunter had a horse that was a horse of power. There are no such horses nowadays.

One day the hunter was riding in the woods, when he noticed all the birds were silent. He wondered at the silence, until he came across a big curved feather lying in his path. It glistened like a flame of the sun, for it was a feather of gold.

Then he knew why the birds were silent, for this golden feather was from the burning breast of the great firebird.

Suddenly the horse of power spoke: 'Do not pick up the flaming feather. If you pick it up you will be sorry, for you will know trouble and you will learn the meaning of fear.' The young hunter hesitated; he did not wish a greater knowledge of trouble, but if he presented it to the King, surely he would be rewarded, for no King had such a feather.

Eventually he decided to pick up the golden feather, and he took it to the King. The King said: 'Thank you, a shining feather from the burning breast of the great firebird is a wonderful thing. But a single feather is not a fit gift for a King. Now, the *whole* bird would be a fitting gift. Surely any man who can find me a single feather can bring me the great firebird itself? I command you to do this, on pain of death!'

The hunter, weeping bitter tears, went and told his horse who said, 'I told you so. But fear not, grieve not. This is not trouble yet—the real trouble lies ahead!'

(Edited and adapted from *Russian Fairy Tales*, pp. 494-497 and
Men and the Water of Life, pp. 209-215)

The performance had kept our attention rapt; now we were to find our personal points of entry to the story. I had a vague suspicion that I was not in possession of a horse of power, as the hunter was from the start. But I was struck by the first glimpse of the feather. This fascinating, scintillating object of beauty was almost irresistible. It gleamed up at me in my mind's eye, daring to be picked up.

The story warned that such moments of inspiration do not come cheaply, that if we see something we greatly desire, and decide to follow it, then we will know trouble and the meaning of fear. The inspiration may be given as a gift, but to follow that inspiration to its source will be to risk burning and death. This was the passion in a man that leads him into danger. It is the testosterone rush that leads a youth towards destruction if there is no king to direct him towards the appropriate expression of his desire. Young men instinctively seek this danger, in fights, fast cars, and drugs, if they cannot get it anywhere else. The Gisu people of Uganda call this drive "Litima", which Michael Meade translated as:

> ... the violent emotion peculiar to the masculine part of things that is the source of quarrels, ruthless competition, possessiveness, power-drivenness, and brutality, and that is also the source of independence, courage, upstandingness, and meaningful ideals.

A sort of "no pain—no gain" idea, but with the stakes somewhat higher. This would read, "No risk of death—no meaningful life." Were there such enticing, danger-ridden golden feathers on the paths our lives had taken so far? Had we picked them up or left them there?

Theatre had been a golden feather in my life, dangerous to pick up, not least because of my parents' success in that field, but which did inspire me and fill me with longing. But the side of theatre which I desired most was the ritual side, what Peter Brook calls "holy theatre," the themes and performances that can create change in those who witness it. And this side I had not actively pursued. I had waited for fallen feathers I could pick up with ease, rather than face the danger of pursuing the whole bird. A sense of purpose perhaps, but permanently on hold, and lacking the passion to spur it on. In the story's terms there was no King around to demand more.

In the inner world this King can be defined as sitting at the center of the psyche, in charge of the whole realm. He knows what we really want in our lives. When the King sees the opportunity to find purpose, he threatens death, because missing the chance is a kind of death anyway. One of William Blake's "Proverbs from Hell" says: "Sooner murder an infant in its cradle Than nurse unacted Desires. . . ." This may not sound politically correct, but it made awful sense. An unacted desire has to be suppressed—and an inner creative child is smothered.

Some men thought that we shouldn't be encouraging this desire, because many male desires are downright destructive. James Hillman, on the tape "Men and the Life of Desire," makes clear distinctions between the desire we were referring to, as opposed to wants or needs. He describes them as stages of a maturing process, with need as the earliest, most childish form of longing. A baby needs its mother, needs help, needs food, needs love; and can't do anything to get them himself. Want is still selfish, but more independent. A teenager wants a car, wants a girl, wants experience, wants money; and can take steps to get them. Need has to ask for it, want can reach for it. The fulfilling of want will satisfy the material impulse but will not give the life purpose. Desire is a kind of soul hunger, the wish for something greater to inform one's life. Desire is not mundane or ordinary; it reaches for brilliance, for genius, for beauty, and for exuberance. Metaphorically, desire seeks the golden burning breast of a great firebird.

Other men spoke of the lack of true desire in their lives, and of dropping the feathers they had seen. Without encouragement it is easy to lose inspiration and to let everyday responsibilities put out the fire. As examples tumbled forth, a pall of loss descended over the group. A strange depression that was not without hope, because it was looking for its source.

I was beginning to recognize the feather that I had dropped last year, when I forgot the inspiration found at the first men's workshop. I saw too the stagnation that had followed. As if, indeed, an unseen King had ordered a "death" as penalty for inaction. Maybe this was another chance.

> The hunter now followed the advice of the horse, spread corn on an open field, hid up a tree and waited. Just after dawn the earth began to shake, and the wind to blow. The great firebird flew over, saw the corn, landed, and began to eat. The horse of power, who was also eating in the field, sidled up to the firebird, and stepped on its wing, pinning it to the ground. The hunter jumped down, tied the bird up, and took it to the King. But the King, though pleased, was not satisfied. He ordered the young hunter to go to the edge of the world, find the beautiful Princess Vasilisa, and bring her to him. The penalty for failure would be the hunter's death. The horse once more said, "I told you so. But weep not, fear not. This is still not trouble—the real trouble lies ahead!"

I felt cheated that the horse had done all the work. Why was this brave hunter hiding up a tree? Of course, having decided I didn't have such a horse, I was probably jealous, but as discussion continued, I realized that I wanted the hunter to be the hero. Like

St. George fighting the dragon, I wished to see the hunter in a brazen confrontation with the firebird. But, as Robert Moore and Douglas Gillette point out, the hero is not entirely selfless:

> It is generally assumed that the heroic approach to life, or to a task, is the noblest, but this is only partly true. The Hero is, in fact, only an advanced form of boy psychology . . . it is immature, and when it is carried over into adulthood as the governing archetype, it blocks men from full maturity . . . If we think about the Hero as the Grandstander, or the Bully, this negative aspect becomes clearer . . . The boy (or man) under this power . . . intends to impress others. His strategies are designed to proclaim his superiority and his right to dominate those around him. He claims center stage as his birthright . . .
>
> *(King, Warrior, Magician, Lover: Rediscovering*
> *the Archetypes of the Mature Masculine*, p. 37)

The hunter has, in the horse, a powerful animal instinct that gives him greater maturity. He can employ strategy, hide when necessary, appear the coward to the casual onlooker, but succeed in his task. The hero might impatiently stab the bird through the heart for effect, the mature warrior is patient and uses minimal force.

Somewhere along the line I had become stuck at an immature level, wishing to be the hero but unable to harness the power that served the hunter of the story. At boarding school I would allow myself to be bullied in the changing rooms while quite big enough to win on the sports field. Suddenly I saw a connection between this and an older, often ill father. I had yearned to see a younger, stronger man engaging in the battles of life and (at least occasionally) winning. When I finally spent time with my father he was engaged in a losing battle with death. I saw him slowly but inevitably beaten and I became afraid—afraid of losing any battle I chose to fight, the way I saw him lose his. I ran away from pain, refusing discipline and the Warrior's path. I became the coward hiding in the moral high ground of pretended pacifism, while anger grew beneath the surface.

The hunter set off on his horse, armed with a golden tent and vintage wines. He traveled to the edge of the world, pitched his tent and waited. The Princess Vasilisa came to visit, drank wine, looked into his eyes and fell asleep. The hunter took her back to marry the King, but she refused, unless the hunter returned to the edge of the world, and brought her the wedding dress hidden in a casket under a large stone at the bottom of the sea. The King ordered the hunter to perform this task, on pain of death. The horse, as before, reminded the hunter that this was not yet *real* trouble . . .

Again the hunter's patience had worked. He had the courage to set himself up in all his finery as the attractive lover, risking rejection in the pursuit of his task. He was not addicted to a single mode of operation, like many so-called modern heroes. He could shift between different styles of activity, along the lines of the versatile Renaissance man and in stark contrast to the increasing drive for specialization that limits modern men.

We were asked to keep the story in our minds during the afternoon, for we would not return to it until tomorrow. Before lunch we each picked a piece of paper out of a hat. On it was written a name, drawn from an image in the story. Each name would become a small group with whom we were to meet at lunch and other specified times. My group was "The men who look under stones." The whole exercise seemed strange and a little silly at the time, but like so much else this weekend, when I went through my resistance I found a reward waiting on the other side.

At our first small gathering I felt very self-conscious. Here we were, seven strangers sitting at a table, trying to introduce ourselves and discuss our thoughts so far. I managed to get away with a first-name introduction and kept my contribution as brief as possible. I soon regretted this, as it seemed to give license to the next speaker to launch into a lengthy monologue. As he delved ever deeper into the reasons for the sexual failure of his various relationships, I became acutely embarrassed. For a few awful moments I assumed his psycho-babble to be the norm—"This is how we men talk when we get together, get down and get honest . . ." I was ready to head for the car. I looked around the table and saw, with some relief, my discomfort mirrored in other, averted eyes. I pulled my attention back to the speaker and noticed how little he was actually saying. It was all learned, like a speech from a play—his well-rehearsed version of various therapists' ideas about his "problem." Of course, being nice, polite British men, we didn't dare interrupt the bullshit. We maintained the supportive front we felt the situation demanded—and held our frustration firmly in check.

After lunch Jackie and I carefully approached Bly and Meade and suggested they might want a drink later on. They did. So off we shot to a local office, grabbing a quick pint and an even quicker bacon sandwich before returning, all bad breath and innocence, for the afternoon session.

Half the large group now met with Robert Bly in the library for an afternoon of Grief Work. We started with a discussion about the value of descent—the "going down" or "wandering in the wilderness" that had appeared, under one guise or another, in all the fairy tales told at these events. And where Prince Ivan was headed in our tale, in his quest to retrieve the wedding gown from "the bottom of the sea."

In ancient traditions, fire is likened to spirit and goes up (the firebird in the sky) but soul is likened to water and sinks down (the gown at the bottom of the sea). But both directions are needed to balance one another. Always striving upwards can make one a *Puer Aeturnus*, a Peter Pan—evading responsibility while seeking ecstasy and eternal youth. Like Icarus, a person may fly too close to the sun and get burnt. The opposite is sinking down. This is the mood of the Senex, the archetype of the Old Man—cold, heavy, slow, depressive, and serious. Too much time here and you may drown in a sea of sorrows from which you can see no way out. No time spent in the depths at all invites disaster.

MELTING THE STONE

If this Descent is not, at some point, undertaken deliberately, it will be foisted upon us. A mid-life crisis, illness, the sudden death of someone close, an unexpected redundancy or bankruptcy will appear to force us down. My recent failure had been just such a message, which I had steadfastly ignored till now. It seemed Robert Bly had read my thoughts, for he pointed out how difficult it was for someone in the public eye (however marginally) to descend. Association with success increases the pressure to stay "up." This may appease the ego but will not feed the soul, which, as Rainer Maria Rilke contends, works better in defeat:

(*Excerpt from*) THE MAN WATCHING

What we choose to fight is so tiny!
What fights with us is so great!

When we win it's with small things,
and the triumph itself makes us small.
What is extraordinary and eternal
does not want to be bent by us.
I mean the Angel who appeared
to the wrestlers of the Old Testament;
when the wrestlers' sinews
grew long like metal strings
he felt them under his fingers
like chords of deep music.

Whoever was beaten by this Angel
(who often simply declined the fight)
went away proud and strengthened
and great from that harsh hand,
that kneaded him as if to change his shape.
Winning does not tempt that man.
This is how he grows; by being defeated, decisively,
by constantly greater beings.

(*Selected Poems of Rainer Maria Rilke,* translated by Robert Bly)

Robert Bly defined four images for descent. "The Way Down and Out" would be a deliberate decision to drop down in social status, to examine yourself and the world from the bottom side up. "Working with Ashes" was taken from "Iron John," when the youth works in the kitchen. This involves raking one's past experiences to see what ancient burnt-out childhood material is getting in the way of the fire. "Learning to Shudder" was about gaining compassion; increasingly difficult in a media-dominated world so inured to violence and death. (The average British child has seen 11,000 deaths on screen by the time he leaves school.)

But the one that caught my breath was: "Moving from the Mother's House to the Father's House." This was the second stage of traditional masculine development, the separation from the mother and the bonding with the father. Since most of us weren't able to achieve this at the "recommended" age of seven, we have to face it later on—and the longer we leave it the tougher it will be. As Bly said, "The effort to move over to the father's house is slow, lonely, and difficult work; every man must accomplish it by and for himself . . ."

Up until this minute I had gotten away with complaining about this missed stage; now I saw there was something that could be done about it. Typically for a male still in the mother's house, I had been waiting for someone else to do it for me.

If, as is often the case, there is no active father around to help this move, the boy will have to trick mother into letting him go. Her natural instinct fights the loss of the son, while the well-trained nice boy waits to be told to go. Mother can rarely bring herself to throw him out of her nest because she knows the boy must "die" as a son in order to be "born" as a man.

The boy may not want to go anyway. He is safer and more comfortable in the mother's house than anywhere else in the world. But when this boy becomes successful, if at all, it is for mother, often using the achievements of his parents rather than earning his own way. It was a trap I knew only too well. Even now I appeared firmly entrenched in the mother's house, heading back into the West End with a play whose primary attraction was her presence. What's more, by running away from father and his influence, I had given myself the perfect excuse for not having anywhere else to go.

Hamlet was given as a literary example of the boy caught in the mother's world and unable to trust the father. I remembered my father had subtitled his film of *Hamlet* "the tragedy of a man who couldn't make up his mind." And here I was—unable to make up my mind to trust the father and enter his house.

Even the talk of descent had seemed to pull us down into a heavy, depressed mood. Now we would try and work with it. We gathered in two circles, one inside the other, to perform a Sufi grief chant. The circles moved in opposite directions while slowly intoning ancient Turkish words. We were asked simply to look into the face of each man passing us in the other circle, and allow the grief we felt to seep into the muscles of our face. At first our British reserve prevailed, "stiff upper lip" battling against the very essence of the exercise. I was tight with tension, still happier directing rather than participating. Brief moments of empathy with other, pained faces mingled with worry—was I doing it right?

Apparently not, for after a few moments Bly stopped us and singled out an elderly looking man as the only face expressing true grief. He asked us each to look into this particular face. I felt still more uncomfortable. Was this poor man to be exhibited like a teacher's pet, applauded for good "grief work?" But the man in question had none of my qualms, and was able to look long and deep into every eye while the intense feeling of grief continued to emanate from his being.

Our moment of connection came—I locked into his steel-gray eyes and stony face. It seemed absolutely sculpted—lines chiseled into skin as though acceptance of life's inevitable harshness had allowed experience to engrave itself on his face. We moved back into our circles and continued with the exercise, but this brief confrontation had shifted something inside me. I felt an inward, downward movement—a pianist scaling down minor chords. A heavy, damp, low feeling, but not depressed; curiously open to deeper resonances with each returning pair of eyes. For these few moments I swam in a sea of grief—not tearful but weighty, bathing in sorrow.

As the exercise drew to a close I shut my eyes and saw in front of me a stone statue of a young boy. There was something familiar about it but I couldn't figure out what. The picture faded but its memory remained—a negative image held in front of the retina. I tried to shake it off as the session ended.

"The men who look under stones" gathered again. One bright spark suggested we talk about why our title was the "right" one for us to have picked out of the hat. I inwardly groaned at the thought of hearing a load of forced connections with stones—until I came up with my own. I suddenly recognized the statue as one I had given to my parents at Christmas two years previously and spoke about this being the stone I had to look under . . . but no more thoughts were forthcoming, and I lapsed into moody silence.

Later on, after a hurried dinner and a silent vow to murder any kidney-bean grower I met, I walked out onto the immaculate forecourt lawn. Other images arose seemingly of their own accord: my son's face—an ancient dream of attacking my mother—my one performance in *Time and the Conways*—these and other undefined pictures floated in my mind. I knew they were linked, but I didn't know how—yet.

I regained my seat in the ballroom for an evening session of "community time," quivering with anticipation and cold. Those who felt a need could now speak freely of "what was most pressing in their lives." Gradually men opened up to share the thoughts and feelings brought up during our twenty-four hours together (it seemed much more). A couple of speakers went off on weird tangents and were sharply interrupted by Bly and Meade. This was a time for "speaking from the heart," not for waffle or polemic. I wished I had known that at lunch. Some were very moving, especially those who obviously struggled for the courage to stand up in the first place, and then battled nobly with unfamiliar emotional language. Finally, I gathered the strength to speak, driven mainly by the fear that if these thoughts were not publicly witnessed they might disappear and die, as they had last year.

I started speaking of a dream I had had as an eight-year-old boy, of jumping out from behind a bush and sticking a knife in my mother's back. The next night I had told my mother the dream. Tears sprang to her eyes. I was immediately overcome by waves of intense guilt, I pleaded for forgiveness, saying how sorry I was, of course I didn't want to kill her, and I'd never dream it again . . .

Now I could see that the dream had been trying to prompt the necessary "death" in the mother/son relationship. But there had been no male energy around to support a move out of the mother's house. My father was in a preliminary skirmish with death—hospitalized with cancer. Somewhere I had decided it was not safe to move into his house—after all, he might die and I would be left alone. So when confronted by the painful seduction of a mother's tears, I quickly ran back into her house and shut the door.

These essential developmental stages are not skipped without sacrifice. I had given up some of my feeling nature, and some of my adventurous spirit. I would receive continued maternal protection but at a cost. Something inside was turned to stone.

Two years ago I had given a small stone statue of a boy to my parents, thinking it a playful reminder of my son. Now I saw it as the stone child in me; a physical symbol of my petrification.

Currently I was directing my mother, in some way reversing roles—as a director "parents" a production—but still I did not feel free. The play was about a family with no father, ruled by an occasionally cruel matriarch, who keeps her eldest son firmly under her thumb. And, on one notable occasion, I had stepped into mother's shoes; literally playing her part, becoming her understudy.

Two things suddenly and forcefully became clear. I now had to move out of the mother's house and towards the father, even if he could only offer a ghostly hand to guide me. The missed step had to be rectified in order to proceed towards independent manhood. And the energy I would need to complete this move was locked within an unfeeling stone child. Only a warming of the cold stone back into life would release the strength I sought.

I sat down, trembling with the intensity of the recognition, and the knowledge of the task that lay ahead.

The remaining community time went by in a blur, followed by drumming and dancing. Halfway through the festivities, Robert Bly indicated that I should move into the center of the space and dance. I tried to shrink away, to pretend that I had not understood him, but he persisted in his gestures until I moved nervously forward. He smiled at me, a supportive smile that gave encouragement rather than affection. I nodded back in acknowledgment, a tacit acceptance of trust. Here was a man who didn't seem to want anything from me, did not seek to control me or limit my actions, yet was offering advice. He was asking me to dance. So I did.

I began pounding my legs into the wooden floor, releasing the pent up energy of the day, seeking some physical confirmation that the absurd parade of images I had seen had meaning. Other men moved forward, adding their own response to my ungainly rhythm. The floor became a seething mass of flailing limbs urged on by the insistent beat of twenty drums.

As I continued to move, instinctively, wildly, I engaged in an age-old inner dialogue. A critical voice inside my head was trying to deny the impact of the day: "This is all bollocks. You'll be fine. You don't need any of this crazy stuff. Look at you for God's sake. You're jumping about like a moron. Don't trust anybody. They'll only use you . . ." It must have been some voice developed years before, a necessary defense to protect me from the trappings of fame and from sorrow, which had now become an impediment. Somehow I had to remember that what was happening was important; too important to forget.

I looked around the room, saw Robert chatting to Jackie in a corner, and decided. I would ask Jackie to join me in starting a small men's group. Some tangible effort to keep the process alive. I closed my eyes, as if to seal the decision, and allowed the heat in the room to enter my body. I was myself and at the same time curiously not myself. I felt stronger than usual, and freer. This was the energy I would need to shatter stone; this strength a taste of what I would have to store up myself.

The dancing seemed endless, but sometime later, as if at a single stroke, the floor ceased its pounding and the circle collapsed inwards, each man supporting his neighbors. Sounds began to emerge, droning moans, joyful shrieks, serene hums, animal calls and pangs of anguish—each release adding to the vocal frenzy. It went on and on, each fading cadence drowned by further waves of noise. At the end I was hoarse, exhausted, drained, and triumphant. Much too tired to sleep, Jackie, myself, and a few others retired to a secluded room to sing (well, croak anyway) and drum on tables well into the night.

When I at last staggered into my dorm I reflected on the day. It had been powerful, but it was not because of any one particular person or activity. It was a combination of the ritual exercises and the shared determination to push ourselves within this protected environment. For me it was not the teaching that was the revelation, but what had arisen from my own imagination. It was as if some ancient tribal memory had been stirred and finally responded.

The next morning was the last session of the weekend. We reassembled in the ballroom, now looking strange and cold after the heated excesses of the previous night, and continued the fairy tale:

> The horse and the hunter returned to the edge of the world. The horse came across a king crab on the beach and put a hoof on its back. In exchange for his life, the crab summoned all the crabs in the sea to find the casket under the stone that contained the wedding dress.
>
> They duly found it; the hunter returned to his kingdom and presented the dress to the Princess. She promptly declared she still would not marry the King . . . unless the hunter was made

to climb into a cauldron of boiling water. The King agreed to this request, and so ordered the cauldron be made ready. The hunter was given permission to say farewell to his horse. The horse admitted that this did indeed look like trouble . . . but advised the hunter not to wait to be carried to the cauldron by the King's men but to run and jump in himself.

This the hunter did, sinking under the boiling water three times but finally emerging stronger and better looking than before. The King decided the cauldron must be a good thing, and he too jumped in, but disappeared and was not seen again until the cauldron was drained and his body removed for burial. So the hunter married the Princess Vasilisa and became King of the realm . . .

In the light of our work on descent the previous afternoon, it felt as though the gown held some lost magical properties, without which the marriage would not be real. Journeying into the depths could release a wedding dress for the soul. But if we cannot fully enter into grief and sorrow maybe we also cannot fully love and honor ourselves or our partner. A quote of Blake's at the end of *Time and the Conways* says:

Joy and woe are woven fine
A clothing for the soul divine;
Under every grief and pine
Runs a joy with silken twine.
It is right it should be so;
Man was made for joy and woe;
And when this we rightly know,
Safely through the world we go . . .

The hunter has to enlist more help and of a different kind. The crab, a lowly creature, walking slowly backwards or sideways, has a shell able to withstand the pressure of the depths. This ability was likened to therapy. We had to find someone with a skill for looking under stones in the past and finding the beautiful clothes, rightly ours, which have been buried for a long time. As Michael Meade pointed out, "Therapy, when successful, happens under pressure, in a dark place, for a limited amount of time."

I had a brief, unwelcome intuition that I would require this kind of assistance to look under the stone I had found. The men's group, if I could get it together, could aid the move to the father's house, but it would take a different energy to release the child in the stone. I shrugged the thought away. One intended commitment was quite enough for one weekend, thank you.

Anyway, there were more pressing matters at hand, like trying to understand the end of the story. The death of the old King must be inevitable. The hunter would never be independent with someone else ordering him around all the time, even if it had been an essential experience. The statement from last year came into my head, "A boy cannot become a man until the day his father dies . . ." Maybe this was a variation on the same theme, "A man cannot become a King until the day the old King dies . . ." In successful male development a boy moves from Mother to Father to Mentor to independence (contact with one's own inner King). Each stage demands the risk of death, but if successful, results in the death of a dependent relationship. The cauldron that the King/Father prepares for us seems life-threatening, but when willingly jumped into, proves life-enhancing. In any case, the story seems to say, it is the only way to become King/Father of our own realm.

Robert Bly suggested some ways to activate the positive inner King. Read biographies of men we feel have some kingly qualities, who have made changes, rediscovered sweetness. Read and write poems about the powerful, creative masculine and put ourselves in positions of leadership where we have to use it.

In order to access King energy we would need "a room" in our heads that was fit for a King to inhabit. This place in the psyche, however, occupies the same space as Father. He is first tenant in the room of masculine authority. If, as most men present readily admitted, they had little positive Father experience, this room would be in a state of neglect. Before a mentor or King would be remotely interested in us we would have to clean up this room, probably redecorate, maybe even rebuild it, brick by brick. If we don't, the current cultural distrust of older men in positions of authority will lead to a dangerous distrust of inner male authority. The inner King will be rejected along with Nixon, Bush, Maxwell, Major, et al.

The work starts with the Father. If we insist on dismissing and blaming him for our troubles, we will simply not have the space to welcome first the mentor and then the inner King. The room will be occupied with the Father's shadow—the demons we attribute to him that then return to haunt us. This is not to whitewash the bad side of the father; we could, Bly suggested, build an extension, so we have one room for the good side, one for the shadow. That would at least be honest.

As we gathered on the lawn outside for a lengthy circular good-bye, I finally accepted that I could run away no more. I had tried to escape paternal influence and the intrusive fingers of his fame, but I had been running in the wrong direction. I was back where I started, standing by his ghostly form. I did not know what demons I would have to face, or what unsuspected blessings lay along the way, but I was heading towards my father's house.

Chapter Six

A Giant Leap for Boy Kind

The next few months were spent tiptoeing around the stone child, trying to breach the rigid defenses to see what lurked within. When some of his secrets began to emerge, far from the joy of release I had anticipated, I moved into depression and anger, and underwent a total humor bypass. I was well and truly in the forest and could not see the wood for the seemingly endless trees. Moments of clarity were soon overwhelmed by confusion. It was all I could do to keep the spark of inspiration alight.

The dreams that emerged and the memories painstakingly dredged to the surface brought with them the emotions I had experienced as a boy. I sought to blame everyone else for what had happened to me. Luckily I found sufficient support to prevent myself from staying with the blame for that would have been to fail again. But not to go through this stage at all would have been to remain inside the mother's house. I had to find good enough reasons to leave that place, for it was no longer the comforting womb I sought. And I had to look at some of the demons around the father's house, in order to face my fear of the place I must now approach.

MELTING THE STONE

A couple of days after our return Jackie and I met with Robert Bly and Michael Meade and were asked to take over the organization of their events in England. We were worried about becoming administrators rather than participants, but agreed to watch and learn during the coming year. We would help with the set up and see if we could manage it in the future without losing the personal impact we had enjoyed/endured so far. And we would try to travel to the United States to see how things were done over there.

Then Robert said he wanted to take a break next year and suggested other men who could teach in his place. We argued against his absence. Most of the men this year had come for his poetry and storytelling skills, few simply because it was a men's event. Anyway, his particular talent lay in getting us true Brits out of our heads for a while, and undermining the stiff upper lip. He acquiesced; whether from his own sense of responsibility or our relentless flattery I'm not sure, but we breathed a sigh of relief as the meeting ended.

Jackie and I retired to a pub for a post-mortem, and I broached the subject of setting up a small men's group. He agreed it had become unavoidable in the wake of the last event, and we started to discuss possible invitations. But we soon ground to a halt, unable to agree on criteria. Ideally we would both know the prospective members, but we didn't have enough mutual friends. The only way to vet them was to have them join; but then if we didn't get on, what would happen? The threat of failure in a venture we both felt important was too fearful to contemplate. We took a rain check.

Later, it became apparent that we were trying to avoid the very fear it is necessary to face in such an enterprise—the unknown. Over-cautious selection might feel safe but would lead to eventual stagnation.

Events were to overshadow this first effort to bring the commitment made in a ritual space out into the world. I was still open to the subtle energies stirred up by the last workshop, and circumstances I would normally have taken in my stride slipped in to shake a vulnerable core.

The first occurred during an interview my mother and I gave to the *Independent on Sunday*. We were in the bar at the Theatre Royal, Brighton, where *Time and the Conways* was playing the penultimate week of its tour, before heading to the Old Vic for a London run. Joan was naturally bearing the brunt of the questions, and I was listening politely as the interviewer asked her about the importance of theatre and family. Her answer came smoothly back, "Well, of course, I love my family, but the theatre is my life." There it was, so simply said, a straight "A" in the Ethics of Showbusiness exam. My rational brain would have understood it as good interview patter, but my rational brain was on vacation. I froze in my chair, feeling the color rush to my cheeks in shame, and braced myself for what must surely follow. This man would turn to me and ask, "How does that make you feel as her son?" But he didn't. He nodded and moved onto bigger game; unwanted questions about marriage to Laurence Olivier.

I was left with a growing inner coldness, as if someone had opened a window onto an Arctic wasteland. Icy air rushed around me as I struggled not to cry out, to shout, "You don't mean that, please say you don't!" Of course, in many ways it was confirmation of what I had intuited long ago. Even though my adult mind appreciated her right to work, to fulfill her own desires, and would not have wanted a frustrated housewife at home anyway, the mind of the child had never understood it, had always wondered what could be more important than time spent together.

Gradually, I clawed myself out of the child's skin, and donned protective professional armor. The efficient caring director took over, and I was grateful to feel familiar numbness close around an aching heart, stifling its plaintive cries for attention. Unable to combat the inherited, resented drive, I too turned my energies to the work at hand, forgot husbandly assurances to return home early and help Shelley with our children. I stayed to see the show, gave copious notes and returned to our shared country cottage at midnight, along with half the cast, for a late, drunken supper.

By the time we had eaten, woken the children up three times, and wobbled off to bed, I found my wife—not in a good mood. I defended myself vigorously, unaware how deeply and suddenly I had fallen into the showbiz ethic myself. Maybe the child had needed respect from its mother, and figured it could only be won through dedicated work. After a dangerously heated argument in which I fully maintained my shaky ground, Shelley posed one of those unbearably fair questions, "When are you going to be able to put as much effort into your family as you do into people you work with?" I blustered for a bit, but then withdrew, to sulk and sleep alone.

I woke early and went to walk off my hangover around the garden, ending up by the statue of the stone boy. As I gazed into his expressionless eyes, I felt a penny drop. I could not go on trying to do it alone. I would have to find some therapist or professional counselor who could accompany me on the treacherous journey into the past to meet the child whose stony representation I now faced. I had been fully determined to break habitual patterns, but just last night had fallen into them without even knowing it. It was as if there was a computer program running me, beyond my conscious control. I needed an expert to help me see what the program was and, hopefully, disengage it.

Inevitably, work prevented me from acting on this decision for a while. A flurry of activity accompanied the London opening of *Time and the Conways*, interrupted briefly for my twenty-ninth birthday celebrations, at which Shelley presented me with the complete works of Swiss psychoanalyst Alice Miller, just so I wouldn't forget.... But once the play was up and running I was able to spend more time at home, reacquaint myself with our children, talk with Shelley about the ramifications of entering analysis, and head into Miller country.

Alice Miller believes that most problems encountered in adulthood have their root in the practices used to rear the child, often in the mistaken belief that such practices are for the child's own good. She maintains that those who never question their upbringing and joke about early suffering "form the hidden source of new and sometimes very subtle humiliation for the next generation" (*The Drama of Being a Child*, p. 92). Although the wounds inflicted on the child can never be healed as the adult, the sting can be taken out of them. Under the right therapeutic circumstances, such feelings can be uncovered, re-experienced and then released:

> Surprisingly, it was the child in me, condemned to silence long ago, abused, exploited, and turned to stone—who finally found her feelings and along with them her speech and told me, in pain, her story.
>
> (*The Drama of Being a Child*, p. xiii)

The recurrence of the stone image spurred me on. I was not alone. Soon after I had a strange dream which I remembered with unusual clarity:

> Workmen are excavating a deep hole in the garden of the country cottage. They find a wild ape in an underground chamber, and report it to my mother, who orders them to blow it up. When I find out about it, the ape has been killed, but I want to go down the hole and at least see the dead body for myself.
>
> I climb down, but when I reach the bottom, I see two tunnels in front of me. One leads to where the dead ape lies, the other to a pub. I decide to go to the pub, and have a drink first. But when I have finished my drink, I have forgotten about the ape. I go out of a side entrance and find myself standing on a street, opposite the stage door of the Old Vic . . .

I awoke excited by the dream. I immediately associated the ape with the wild man, and thought that this image was showing me what I had suspected before, that some spontaneous, creative side of me was buried, dormant, perhaps dead. And that my drinking was designed to forget the pain of this fact. More worrying was the idea that this death had been ordered by my mother, and I had been unable to stop it. Alice Miller did not make me feel better:

> Accommodation to parental needs often (but not always) leads
> to the 'as-if personality' (Winnicott has described it as the 'false
> self'). This person develops in such a way that he reveals only
> what is expected of him . . . He cannot develop and differentiate
> his 'true self,' because he is unable to live it . . . Understandably,
> these patients complain of a sense of emptiness, futility, or
> homelessness, for the emptiness is real. A process of emptying,
> impoverishment, and partial killing of his potential actually took
> place when all that was alive and spontaneous in him was cut
> off . . . These people have often had dreams in which they expe-
> rience themselves as partly dead.
>
> (*The Drama of Being a Child*, p. 27-28)

I had ended up tamely waiting outside the stage door of the
Old Vic, which was not only where my mother and sisters were
currently playing in *Time and the Conways*, but where my parents
had been working much of the first ten years of my life. Maybe I
had had to be tamed in order that they could pursue their work
effectively.

I recalled at age five being taken out of a mixed easy-going primary school, and sent to a strict, all boys school, ruled by an old
colonel deeply attached to the cane. I went because I was "in se-
vere need of discipline," and lived with four years of fear. When I
left I was a nice, kind, well-mannered boy—no apes in sight.

I did not know how to pursue these thoughts further, but recognized that the dreamer was not in control. Both the mother figure
and alcohol held sway over him. He could not yet get to the ape by
himself. This proved the final spur. I called a friend trained in
Jungian analysis and asked him to recommend an older male analyst who was in touch with his emotions, and consequently called
a Dr. David Kay.

In-between the phone call and the initial consultation, I reopened
the *Shirley Valentine* tour in Derby. On the train up, I watched the
landscape rush by and wondered what the hell I was letting myself in for.

TREES IN WINTER

The winter trees stretch out
their frail fingers
to touch the winter sun
which fades inexorably from their sight;

The upstanding branches, braced against weather, wait patiently
for spring—
take defenestration without remorse, and glory in skeletal nu-
dity.

The winter trees seem to whisper:
"This is what I am, and ever will be.
I dare to show what's underneath.
Do you...?"

As I drove on the first of many subsequent journeys to Finchley
Central, I was filled with dread. Could I go through with it? All my
life I had learned *not* to say what I really felt, *not* to explain what
was really going on. This middle-class basic training was reinforced
on the parade ground of Fame, where every comment has to be
pre-screened for press safety, every stranger treated with suspicion,
guilty until proved innocent. And here I was about to try and talk
to a complete stranger about . . . everything.

I arrived at the door and was greeted by Dr. Kay, a kindly looking middle-aged man, who showed me into a small office. I flinched
at the sight of the couch and quickly sat down in one of the two
black leather chairs. If I had chosen the couch he would surely have
thought me mad.

Now I felt like a *Jeopardy* contestant with amnesia. What were
the right answers? What was the subject anyway? Me. Oh, shit!
What the hell would I say? How long would it take? What would
happen if he rejected me? And if I was accepted, how would I know
it was not because of my father, yet again! I had no idea how to

109

express these fears, so I didn't. I remained awkward and aloof, politely relating edited highlights of my life.

"Conceived in New York—born in Brighton—mother unconscious when born—breast fed five months—two working parents—brought up with nannies—sent to strict school—Dad's cancer. Boarding school—time with Dad "only when he was too ill to work" —at fifteen fell in love with girl at school (one friend described this as a "Rover-Juliet" relationship) —failed Oxbridge—college in Los Angeles. Started work as theatre director—met future wife—got married—back to England—had children—father died—unable to grieve—unable to balance work and family life—increasing sense of immaturity, lack of control and confusion."

Much to my disappointment my monologue had failed to produce a miraculous cure, but I had got on with David and we agreed to start regular sessions.

The morning of our next meeting I had a dream in which my first, unrequited love appeared. The helpless adoration was there in the dream, as it had been at age fifteen. It felt like a cue, so I talked to David about the relationship. The painfully naive yearning, increasing possessiveness and refusal to see that these feelings would not be reciprocated. When the "forgive me and forget me" letter came, I was torn apart; fantasy finally forced to face reality. I worked for months to rid myself of the pain of a heart cut in two. I could even recall the actual moment of freedom; I was on a bus for some school trip, looking out of the window. Suddenly, as if by magic, the hot dagger was withdrawn. The lack of feeling it left was a blessed relief; soothing, light, cool.

Another memory bell began ringing. I tracked it down. Three years ago, Shelley and I had taken my father to a homeopathic doctor who specialized in applied kinesiology. Using muscle testing to ask the body questions, he had determined that Dad's series of near crippling illnesses stemmed from "a massive trauma to the heart" suffered in March 1949. The specificity of his dating staggered me; and when Larry professed not to remember any problems from that year, I resolved to do a little detective work with his autobiography. Now I found the relevant page again, which concerned the beginning of the end of his marriage to Vivien Leigh:

> But—and please God let that be the most appallingly biggest 'but' in this little lifetime—one day early in spring 'I heard a maid complaining' . . . It came like a small bolt from the blue, like a drop of water. I almost thought my ears had deceived me: 'I don't love you any more.'
>
> I felt as if I had been told that I had been condemned to death. The central force of my life, my heart in fact, as if by the world's most skillful surgeon, had been removed. It left me agasp but not gasping; it was as if I had been rendered forever still inside, like a fish in a refrigerator . . . a crowned head after the execution.
>
> I could only keep it bottled up in myself and, as Vivien had suggested, carry on as if nothing had changed.
> I supposed I would learn to endure this coldly strange life, so long as I never looked to be happy again . . . There would still be the lantern of my work, though its flame seemed all but burned out; I would have to find other means of inspiration, this one's throne was empty.
>
> (*Confessions of an Actor*, p. 172-173)

Had I inherited this "heartlessness?" Did the cold strange feelings come from him? As far as I could tell, he had never quite recovered from this loss. He suppressed it; for several years acting a part in a marriage that was dead. Unable to grieve, his emotions were channeled into public work not private life. I now firmly donned my Sigmund Holmes hat, and with more than a little voyeuristic glee, continued to search for psychological clues.

I found out that my father's history of rejection had started early. He often maintained that he was unwanted by his father, a hardworking Anglican priest, who already had a son and a daughter, and thought Larry an unnecessary extra mouth to feed. Larry had become his mother's favorite, cosseted and pampered, until she died unexpectedly when he was only twelve. Her dying wish was that he be sent to a particular school, but his father decided it would be too expensive and sent him to another, where he learned to put his energies into acting. Maybe placing a fictitious character between him and the world gave him the security he could not find elsewhere:

> . . . the one inside moves back, and the hands touch nothing, and are safe.
>
> (Robert Bly, from "Snowbanks North of the House")

I was becoming aware of certain patterns in his life that seemed to be engraved on mine. As the educator Herbert Pestalozzi wrote, "You can drive the devil out of your garden but you will find him again in the garden of your son." (Thanks a bunch.) My father already had a son, and when my mother became pregnant, wanted a daughter. I had experienced a loved one's rejection and responded with similar "open heart surgery." Was there a similar withdrawal of parental affection? Obviously not in the same terms or with the same force, but a memory surfaced which, under emotional scrutiny, seemed to contain a "little death."

As a small child, sleeping in the basement of our large house in Brighton, I was convinced that man-eating crocodiles lived at the end of the corridor. Whenever I woke up I would listen and, on the slightest sound, run terrified into the nanny's room for comfort. On the nanny's nights off my parents would listen on an intercom from their upstairs bedroom and come down when necessary. After a while it became obvious that this had become a nightly habit and an unwarranted disruption to the household—my father was once heard to mutter on his way down the stairs that he'd "rather play Othello twice, any day." And so a plan was hatched.

The rest of this story became a popular family tale, though I have only the vaguest memory of it myself. Apparently, one night when the nanny was out, my parents decided to stay in the nanny's room but locked all the doors. As expected I rose in the middle of the night, tried to enter the nanny's room, couldn't, tried to go upstairs, couldn't, and started crying. And carried on crying—for about an hour. During this time my mother, listening on the other side of the door, often wanted to give in, come out and comfort me, but my father nobly restrained her from this temptation—for my own good.

Eventually I stopped and said feebly into the space around me, "How can I keep on crying if no one is going to come?" When I didn't receive any answer I went back to bed. My nocturnal wanderings ceased. As, maybe, did my faith in a good universe.

Of course, on one level, it was simply effective discipline. My pitiful question had become the punch-line to a sweet story which proved my parents right. If no one came, and the crying stopped, then the disruption was proved unwarranted. A selfish child seeking attention who would now grow up a bit.

But from the child's point of view it was an early lesson in petrification. The question could be rephrased, "How can I go on allowing myself to feel bad if no one is going to come and make me feel better?" The answer, of course, is that I couldn't. As an infant I had been woken up late at night to play with my parents on their return from the theatre. As a child, maybe I was merely continuing this loving routine, except, now, it was rejected. I had to bury this apparently unacceptable need. Unfortunately, as I had recently discovered, it is not possible to bury one feeling (fear, pain, or whatever) and keep all the rest intact. Any one feeling will take a group of others with it. A prime example of "throwing out the baby with the bathwater."

A few more experiences of this nature, including a strict school, and then being sent away to board at the age of ten, and the child realized that a deal was being set up. It would be loved if it didn't express fear, didn't cry, and didn't cause trouble: but it would be "abandoned" if it broke the rules. Any expression of rage against the rules would lead to apparent further punishment—from locked doors to canes to boarding school—until, fearful of final and complete abandonment, rage was banished from consciousness. Whenever a wild ape was found it would be blown up, by paid helpers, but on the instructions of my parents. So I grew up to think it better to have a quick drink, forget about apes, and get on with the important things in life-like theatre.

By now I was on a roll, blaming anyone and everyone, but especially my parents, for everything that had gone wrong in my life. I couldn't help it. Every time I scraped the surface, I found an underlying pool of childish anger. Far from growing into mature manhood, I felt I was regressing, getting smaller by the day. I had to try and take courage from Alice Miller:

> The free expression of resentment against one's parents . . . provides access to one's true self, reactivates numbed feelings, opens the way for mourning and—with luck—reconciliation . . . It is an essential part of the process of psychic healing.
>
> (*For Your Own Good*, p. 251)

I was hoping I would not become stuck in the resentment. However important it was to undergo, there was something sticky about it, ugly and dependent. And there could be no easy external confirmation that I was doing the right thing. I carried on, because in the words of an old Scottish warrior—I was "in blood steeped so far, that to return were as tedious as go o'er."

A few weeks later, while in Canada remounting *Time and the Conways* and visiting the Henrichs, my Canadian in-laws, I had another dream:

> I am on a train in the front line of a huge battle. I run to the back of the train to get a rifle and ammunition. I come back but the attack is already over and the enemy beaten. A colleague speaks of 'seeing someone run away'—I keep quiet but think myself brave to have faced fire while moving, rather than hiding and waiting, unarmed.

Later I am a lookout at the front of the train, checking for explosives on the track. The train comes to a halt in front of a tunnel. I sense this is the moment for an ambush, so I rush back to a bathroom, put on plastic underpants and grab my rifle . . .

Usually in dreams I run away and hide. But here, though scared, I was ready to face battle. I knew where my gun was and I went to get it, twice. The plastic underpants were a comic reminder of my previous life as a coward, a warning of the fear to come and a sign of a new determination not to be undone by that fear. It seemed to suggest that I was on the right track, albeit not a particularly safe track.

I had recently told my sisters and mother that I was in analysis and, though they were polite enough, I sensed they thought this a rather cowardly way out, either unnecessary or simply running away into blame and self-pity. Now I felt reassured that though I may have been moving backwards—into childhood memories—it was to arm myself for the future.

Meanwhile, back on the men's ranch, Jackie and I had finally beaten off all inner resistance, and were heading for a date with destiny. Or rather we had convinced four other poor bastards to join us for a few men's meetings. Of course, we didn't have a clue where to start, but I had been asked to visit another group and promised to steal any useful ideas.

When I arrived at this meeting I was introduced to six other men, mostly older, mainly in business suits. We started off by listening to a Bly tape, which proved a mistake; the tape machine proceeded to suck any spontaneous energy out of the room and was abandoned half-way through. No one was willing to offer a personal reaction to the topic of "The Naive Male." A few nervous shifts on sofas and the conversation soon drifted to the impending Gulf War. Within ten minutes two of the suits were in a political discussion about oil prices—and I knew I would not be returning.

There was no commitment to a different level of disclosure. Everyday defenses were firmly in place while ego battles were fought between entrenched political allegiances. At the first decent opportunity I made my excuses and left, having discovered only what not to do.

When the evening of our first men's group meeting arrived I was amazed to find that I was not overly fearful. The butterflies in my stomach were in anticipation rather than dread. Of course, I was on "home territory" in Jackie's kitchen and, the way the acceptances had panned out, I had at least met all those due to appear. We had asked everyone to agree to a trial six meetings—after which we could disband, regroup or continue—so we could give it a fair shot.

As the first arrival rang the doorbell I did have fleeting doubts about the sanity of the exercise. I would have to disclose as much as anyone else: but without the safe anonymity of the small group at the last event, or the privacy of therapy. What was I letting myself in for?

It was too late for second thoughts. I opened the door to Jason, then David, Chris, and Howard who joined Jackie and myself for food, drink, and intros. We went around the table, first saying a little about ourselves in general, and then being more open about the motivation for our presence. After retiring to the sitting room we settled down for more in-depth discussion; how we felt about being here and what we wanted to get out of it.

I remember five men (including myself) citing various states of fear while one seemed positively joyful. My God, maybe it didn't have to be all doom and gloom. Would we be able to celebrate our shared masculinity as well as question it?

Behind the apparently calm surface lay, inevitably, many different views of the evening itself. To give a sense of perspective—and the overriding nerves the beginning of such an enterprise evokes— I asked those willing to cast their minds back to the evening of February 20, 1991.

As I watched the first lad trudging despondently across Ladbroke Grove towards my window, I knew that—unless I ran out the back door and kept on running—whatever the reality of men's work it was going to be embracing (if not hugging) me for a long time.

We spent the evening in a shy and tentative semi-gloom, through which our words sporadically blazed. It was like forming a support group to discuss the unlikely escape from an addiction to a particularly vicious tranquilizer. Because of the concussive effect of the 'drug' we could only feebly remember our young lives before addiction, and miserably speculate on life post-addiction.

We ate soup, we drank wine, we mumbled sincerely, but whatever we said, we fucking well meant it, and we survived the terrible experience, to have the best laughs and deepest psychological challenges that a fellow could reasonably withstand. (Jackie)

At that time I was five months through working out my six-month redundancy notice from the job I had had for twenty-seven years. I had just given a large birthday party to celebrate being fifty-five, which was in a way also a farewell—to the well-paid and established person I had been and to my friends. A very close friend had died the night before and I suspected my girlfriend was having an affair (we split a month later). So when I took all of this baggage to our first meeting I was already feeling very uncertain of the future and preparing for change.

I was nervous—I think we all were. There was a lot of talking; where else do you start? But I liked the openness and the willingness to try and be honest. There was a lack of direction, but that must tend to happen in an unled group. I have been in many groups and one of the first questions I ask myself is if I could spend time with these people for the rest of my life. I was very surprised to hear myself answer 'yes'; because I realized that I need not try to be polite and cover up—that things would get difficult (and they did). In a strange way, on really no basis, I felt protected. (Chris)

I was tremendously excited at being invited to join a small men's group (which to me then was an unusual and mysterious gathering) and agitated at crossing this threshold into such irresistible, yet unknown and challenging territory. What's more, this particular group had a direct line of communication to Robert Bly and offered the promise of closeness to the cutting edge of UK men's work.

I recall the reassuring feelings of goodwill and common enquiry at the beginning of our first meeting. I felt honored to be chosen and included, for my maleness and my character. I keenly observed and listened to the other men, exhilarated by the eloquence and poetry of what was expressed, and impressed by the diversity of experience and perspective. I felt a sense of belonging, of being there for who I was. I was eager, keen, and impatient to get down to the nub of our discussions—to go deeply and subjectively into personal and group process. I had a sense that others were not comfortable with my readiness for such direct engagement—and that a more elusive, arm's length interaction would be the norm. Each member's willingness to allow developments varied and I recall, quite early on, having friction and feeling unsafe with some members who held back. (This still continues . . .) (David)

I approached with some trepidation. I had not done anything like this before. My imagination was rampant. This, it was telling me, was going to be bad. Fleeing certainly seemed the best option, but then how was I going to explain my absence . . . and anyway the doorbell was ringing. I resorted to an old but successful defense, get big (i.e. stand at my six and a half feet), say nothing unless it's enigmatic or ambiguous, preferably both, and figure out who is going to get crucified and who is going to do the crucifying: be neither.

I had a few drinks on the principle that this always helps: it didn't, I stayed quiet, but dozy. I remembered playground games which were played until one fool committed too far and then the pack descended on the victim. I looked for allies, trying to see who was to lead and who to trail so I could jostle for medial anonymity, but there seemed some different intent in the clumsy seating negotiation, there was no sharpening of teeth. I sat near the door, just in case.

Someone began to speak, a gentle desperate moment as we let go, beginning the slow magic that is men speaking from the heart, and more importantly, listening there. I hardly noticed the leap I was making. My head was still wary, but I felt we were all in the same boat, trying to row in the same direction. Towards the end of the evening I began to speak . . . (Jason)

Each man seemed to open up, to whatever level they were willing or able, and say things about themselves that I had never heard before, even from the good friends present. As we all, slowly but surely, began to express honest perceptions of our current positions in life, I had a fleeting sense that something had started that would continue. The men gathered, though differing widely in experience and sensibility, did not grate against each other in the ego-bashing way characteristic of most male groupings.We wrapped up at about eleven o'clock on friendly enough terms and everyone agreed to turn up at the next meeting with a poem.

Soon after, I received an announcement for a unique event in America planned for early May. It was to be the first Multi-Cultural Men's Conference where "one hundred men of diverse cultures will gather together for six days in a way that will encourage straight talk, understanding, and community." It had been inspired by Michael Meade. Robert Bly and James Hillman would be there too, joined by Haki Madhubuti, acclaimed African-American poet and essayist; Malidoma P. Somé, an African medicine man and double Ph.D.; Joseph Walker, Tony award-winning playwright; and other assistants in dancing, drumming, and mask making. I was intrigued by the length of the event and the participants—it promised to be even more "initiatory" than a weekend. Many of

these men had contributed to a Multi-Cultural Foundation, Mo-
saic, that would sponsor a large portion of the costs, making it fairly
affordable. I spoke to Jackie and, partners permitting, we agreed to
make this our preparatory expedition.

I expected a week away to be a difficult negotiation with Shelley.
I was aware I was asking a lot before I had effected any major change
at home. But there was already a sense that the work I was starting
had taken some pressure off her, a relief that the weight of my stuff
no longer fell quite so squarely on her shoulders. I was surprised
and grateful to be encouraged to go.

At the second men's group, we started off by reading poems
aloud, and tried to allow spontaneous emotional reactions to surface. Mine was a Rilke poem:

(*excerpt from*) I AM TOO ALONE . . .

I want to unfold.
I don't want to stay folded anywhere,
because where I am folded, there I am a lie.
I want to describe myself
like a painting that I looked at
closely for a long time,
like a saying that I finally understood,
like the pitcher that I use everyday,
like the face of my mother,
like a ship
that took me safely
through the wildest storm of all.

(From *Selected Poems of Rainer Maria Rilke,* translated by Robert Bly)

The nice polite boy I had become was just such a fold, hiding
other potentials behind his concern to be liked. I hoped that this
group could be a space in which to unfold gently, to show things I
would normally be too embarrassed or self-conscious to reveal outside.

For another man, the image of the mother's face had brought up an early childhood rejection. As he began an apparently objective interpretation of this memory, I jumped in, "But how does that make you feel?" A stony look told me it had been an insensitive intrusion. We were creating something that was not "group therapy." This process—as yet deliberately undefined—would involve more than trying to push each others' emotional buttons. If we were to trust each other with deep feelings the "container" of the group would have to be strong enough to hold them first. Particularly without a leader, we needed the weight of more experience; a better knowledge of each other and our wounds.

We continued with no obvious agenda, and no formula or structure to speak of. At the next meeting further questions of trust and fear were raised. We had decided to keep our discussions totally confidential; but those of us with live-in partners were already experiencing problems. "And what happened in your men's group tonight, darling?" —"Oh, you know . . . nothing much," did not inspire the hoped for increase in communication. There had to be a way to divulge something, or inevitable suspicion of separatism and exclusion would become an uncomfortable reality. After heated debate we agreed on a "play it by ear" basis, where subjects could be shared while anonymity given to the source.

By our fourth meeting we came up against a tougher barrier—fear of exposure. Everything in our culture and upbringing teaches us to compete, conquer, and win, and, if and when we lose, to grin and bear it "like a man." We were gathered to honor our defeats, but could we do it without competing with each other through force of habit? Would the group degenerate into an accepted pecking order, with each man sticking to an assigned place in a hierarchy? Already people were slipping into roles. I defined myself as the pushy director, others as the joker, the convoluted thinker, the quiet philosopher, the angry poet, and the happy analyst.

We began to probe our roles. It felt dangerous, because it was talking about the masks we wore rather than talking through them.

These roles gave us a sense of secure identity without which we felt naked, vulnerable. They enabled us to maintain control, to prevent some imagined fall into chaos. Now we were tempting this chaos. Were there really no limits? Could we say what we really felt about others, to those others? Where would it stop?

A communal fear emerged that "no holds barred" would lead us towards uncontainable rage. Strangely it was not others' anger that was feared as much as our own. If I put down the protective mask I would be unbearably vulnerable to the whims of the other men. If I was hurt when open, I would become terrifyingly angry, perhaps even destructive.

So we maintained a civilized front at least partly to protect others from this potential violence. This was quite a shock. Most of us had been drawn to a men's group through recognizing ourselves as "soft males." But beneath the surface darker energies lurked. When the final details for the Multi-Cultural Conference arrived, Michael Meade's introduction gave good reason for the slow, solid foundation we were engaged in building.

> For thousands of years, men have been killing each other. That's one of the activities that men do, and they generally do it to other men. There's no getting away from it, and we carry it in our blood and in our memories. So whenever a group of men get together, there's this issue: "Is someone going to be killed?" And usually the second question is, "Will it be me?"

I would soon find out.

Chapter Seven

An Englishman Abroad

And so, one sunny afternoon in May, I found myself at the end of a long queue outside a log cabin in the Buffalo Gap Camp for the Cultural Arts, West Virginia. Queuing was to prove the most British thing I did all week.

I was in a state of subdued terror. Rumors that gang leaders from LA and New York had been invited to attend had heightened my event nerves. And this was not a normal event. It had been set up with the aim of trying to confront the anger and fear that men of different races usually avoid—or express through violence. And it was the first of its kind. The organizers had no more idea of what to expect other than the participants.

I was smiling nervously, pathetically, at everyone in sight, but especially at the larger black men who walked by. One man rolled by with bulging muscles and closely cropped hair. I whispered to Jackie something about "being built like a brick shithouse" and "avoiding dark alleys." I watched him walk up to the front of the line, only to be turned away by another tough-looking customer. This man was leaning backwards on a chair, wearing shades, one foot propped up against the door to deny premature entry to the registration hut. I quickly sized up this bouncer/guardian of the threshold as a potential armed gang leader. He turned out to have graduated from the UCLA theater arts department the year before I joined—we had several mutual friends. It was to be that sort of week: preconceptions overturned, prejudice exposed.

After what seemed like a very long time, the sound of drums began to emanate from the log cabin. The black men started slapping thighs to the rhythm, while the white men around me paled further. The realization that a special ceremony was about to start prompted fantasies of Masonic rituals and deeply serious party forfeits. The beat was slow and methodical, but began building in intensity. The door opened and men were allowed inside, but mysteriously only three at a time. Other threes were admitted every few minutes, but the first entrants did not reappear for fifteen minutes. When they did, they picked up their bags in silence and only smiled in response to our questions—leaving the rest of us to fearful imaginings.

By the time I got to the front of the line I was a bundle of nerves. Logical thoughts like "It can't be that bad . . ." were overwhelmed by a cacophony of answers, "But what if it is?" "How the hell do you know," etc. I walked into the darkness with a pounding heart. As my eyes adjusted, a large black hand gently touched my elbow and guided me to a small, blanket-covered booth in a corner. I nervously pulled back the flap and almost laughed with relief to see that a table lamp and three large pieces of paper were the extent of the demons that awaited me. I stepped in and read the headings "Lion Clan," "Snake Clan," and "Heron Clan," with poetic descriptions of each underneath. I knew I was supposed to read each carefully before I made a choice, but as soon as I saw the word "Lion" my mind was made up.

I left the booth to walk tentatively through the middle of a large group of drummers. Lit only by candles, their shadows flickered against the surrounding walls. Would this be the moment of terror? I made it safely to the Lions' registration table, and fished in a bowl to pick my accommodation—Cabin 10. I thought this was all going rather well and prepared for a quick exit. I turned a corner to see some men working around a table. One of them asked me over, handed me a pair of scissors and explained my task of cutting strips of dry plaster of paris—with which we would later make masks—until I could entice "some other sucker" to take over. After an inordinate amount of time—all the men I asked smiled knowingly and kept walking—I got to take my bags to Cabin 10. Some beds had already been chosen and by one stood a large box of food. Was this guy just nervous or had he been here before? Worry turned to joy when Jackie came in with his bags. He had not only chosen the Lion Clan, but picked the same small group. We had had a one in twelve chance of ending up together, but luck was on our side. So far.

About an hour later a bell summoned us to the main meeting room for our first formal gathering where Joseph Walker, one of the main three black teachers, led us in a chant to Ellegba, African god of the crossroads. One of the assistants, Aidoo, a master drummer (trained in the African tradition of musician as spiritual healer), then started a libation ceremony. We could call on the names and spirits of any friends, dead or alive, mentors, ancestors, guardians, or allies to join us and share the water libation, which he would bless and pour into a bowl as a welcome. I was already being pulled into the rituals of a culture that I knew nothing about—I felt terribly alien, but decided the polite thing to do was to shut my eyes and think of England.

The first man to speak launched into a lengthy prayer to Jesus Christ and Almighty God, giving thanks for safe arrival and seeking further protection—he had obviously been unnerved by Ellegba too—and we were swiftly reminded to call out names only. The next speaker welcomed his father, the next called out Malcolm X. I quickly opened one eye, identified the speaker as the black teacher wearing a "By any means necessary . . ." T-shirt, thought, "Oh, shit," and shut it again. More names were called out, repeated by Aidoo as he poured the libation, and so it continued.

I soon realized this was going to take some time and tried to relax. I began to pay attention to the changing energy in the room. As the number of names grew, I found myself drawn to this strange process. It was as if, in some amorphic way, we were breaking down a barrier. Through hearing of those whom others cared about so much, we were no longer simply anonymous, differently colored men, but people with a past; ancestors, family, friends, and loved ones.

I suddenly wanted to join this choir of introduction. I waited until a suitable break, then nervously asked that "my father, Laurence, and my grandfather, Ernest" be invited in. I had to brace myself; but as soon as the words passed my lips I was flooded with warmth. I was glad I had risked invokaying my masculine line. I imagined these spirits floating over the camp, flying through the roof and drinking the libation. And I felt safer, more protected.

The ceremony continued until all those who wished had had their say. We now separated and met our clan leaders. Michael Meade and Jo Walker led the Lion Clan up to a large outdoor dance platform, and spokaye of Lion energy—images of generosity, mercy, and kingliness were balanced with fierceness, laziness, and rage—before setting our next tasks. We were to divide again into our small groups, each of which would be given a large piece of differently colored cloth and a pair of scissors (to do with what we liked), introduce ourselves, and select a group leader. These leaders would meet the event teachers each morning to discuss progress and problems.

So the eight men from Cabin 10 gathered in a corner. I was disappointed to find our group contained only one black man—I didn't want it to be this safe—but not half as disappointed as he was; he spent all his life with white men and came here to meet brothers. A younger man broached the leadership question by suggesting that our leader should be the man who most needed to "find his voice" for some important upcoming project. Since the speaker had just finished telling us how he needed to find his voice for a large upcoming project, I saw this as a devious, male political ploy. To my dismay, the group immediately supported this criterion, which, since I had spokayen of working on large productions already, effectively ruled me out. The only way I could exert influence now would be to foil the young pretender's attempt. So I quickly and confidently nominated the eldest man there, pointing out his upcoming projects while emphasizing the importance of honoring age. No one could reasonably disagree and he was duly elected—leaving me to reflect on my vengeful manipulation at the start of a week requiring trust, openness, and honesty.

"Noble Leader"—as he was soon tagged—then had to decide what to do with our piece of bright red cloth. We ended up with a short strip around our left wrists, with a large piece left over "for later." I regarded our choice with skepticism—they reminded me of hospital tags —and was jealous of the cooler lookaying bandannas some of the other groups had already tied around their foreheads. Since I did not seem to be getting my way in anything much, I sulked and decided the whole idea was silly anyway, like a Boy Scouts expedition.

But as we gathered again for dinner, and I witnessed the proliferation of these cloths—a different color for each small group—I saw that we had been subtly encouraged to forge cross-cultural allegiances. If all the black men had worn red, the white men blue and other races green (for example), it would have been a disaster. But in our group alone we had two Brits, three European Americans, one African American, one Chicano, and one Chinese American—all now identified as "Reds" and belonging together. The fact that this identity was claimed through color was even more startling. Our group was a mini-race; our red a new, shared, color identity. It was not as if other colors had become enemies, but we had become allies. The traditional racial divides we had entered the camp with a few hours ago had already been thrown into tactical confusion.

After dinner the motives and schedules for the event were explained. Michael Meade said that after ten years of men's conferences, at which 99 percent of the participants had been white, the question he had was, "Is this work men's work—or is it white men's work?" There were no real rules at these events but everyone was asked to agree to two things: no physical violence—loud agreement; and no mental breakdowns, "if you've been saving one till now—save it a little longer"—(loud laughter). I joined in the jovial agreement: two days later I would feel that both conditions had been brokayen.

The daily schedule was given out, and sounded safe enough—until four-thirty was announced as the start of an hour for "Intentional Conflict." I felt the hairs on the back of my neck stand up, as I listened to the explanation. "We figure we're all going to get pissed off with each other anyway—we'd like to do it at four-thirty." But the heat was destined to build much sooner. Every night there was to be "community time." Men were invited to speak about "what is urgent in your life right now."

A poem by the African-American poet and writer, Haki Madhubuti—he of the Malcolm X T-shirt—set the tone for what followed:

WHITE ON BLACK CRIME

lately and not by choice
milton washington is self employed.
workin hard
he collects aluminum cans,
pop bottles, papers and cardboard
and sells them to the
local recycling center.

milton washington is an unemployed
master welder who has constantly sought
work in & out of his trade.
he is now seen on benches, in parks,
in garbage cans, leaving well lit alleys
in the evenings pushing one cart
& pulling the other, head to the side
eyes glued southward long steppin homeward.

milton's unemployment ran out 14 months ago
first the car went & he questioned his manhood
next the medical insurance, savings and family
nights out ceased & he questioned his god.
finally his home was snatched & he disappeared
for two days and questioned his dreams
and all he believed in.

milton works a 15 hour day &
recently redefined his life for
the sixth time selecting as his only goal
the housing, feeding & keeping his family
together.

yesterday the payout per pound
on aluminum was reduced by 1/4 cent
as the stock market hit an all time high
& the president smiled through a speech
on economic recovery, welfare cheats & the
availability of jobs for those who want to work.

milton washington has suffered
the humiliation of being denied food stamps,
the laughter and cat calls of children,
the misunderstanding in the eyes of his family
and friends.
milton believed in the american way
even hung flags on the fourth and special days
and demanded the respect of god and country in
his home.

at 1/4 cent reduction in pay per pound
milton washington will have to add
an hour and a half to his 15 hour day.
milton washington, more american than black,
quiet and resourceful, a collector of dreams

cannot close his eyes anymore,

cannot excuse the failure in his heart,
cannot expect miracles in daylight,
is real close, very, very close to hurtin somebody
real bad.

A pall of truth had moved over the group. A man stood up to speak of his work in a drug unit at a large prison. The lost men and boys he dealt with by day haunted him every night. He saw the need for some kind of initiation, "without which males turn to crime . . . we've become a society which preys on older people . . . we don't carry their bags—we take their bags."

Another man worked in a hospice for AIDS babies. "I work with the mothers—I bury the children." When a beautiful black baby had died in his arms a few weeks before he had wanted to run through the streets with the body, shouting, "Lookay what we are doing to the children!" He paused, the emotion he had intended only to relay catching him once more. The room was silent, we held our collective breath. He finished simply, "Where are the fathers? Where are the brothers?"

The last speaker introduced himself as Abati. He didn't think black men were ready to take part in a project like this. "We need to become conscious of our masculinity first, then our families, and then our black communities." And impeding any real progress in this work was an inherited, enforced, lack of self respect: "The consequences of slavery—which haunt my fuckin' ass! The issue is the absence of my manhood and that is a process which will take generations to heal." By now we were running late, the question of the usefulness of an event like this would remain unanswered—tonight.

The next morning Robert Bly and James Hillman opened proceedings. Already there had been a number of comments about the lack of effective fathering. Hillman urged us to imagine the Father in a different way. Having been at men's events for five years, he had witnessed the yearning to be fathered amongst the gathered men, but he had come to distrust the insistence that we all "should have" a nice, good, caring father. And he was getting annoyed with listening to all the complaints when this didn't happen.

> What bridge did your father come over, when you were standing elsewhere, that you didn't see, because of your own need for specific recognition? The more you repeat the complaint, the more you remain a wounded child. Maybe your father blessed you in ways you haven't seen. We focus on our needs and remain sons. But the things you most resent may be gifts. Reflect them one more time. Don't stay angry or you will miss the other benefits…

He stressed that we should not avoid the anger, but if we stayed there, we would remain stuck in the same place we were as a child— as complaining has a childish tone to it. I thought about my recent gleeful parental blame laying, and was grateful to know that it was not the end of the road by a long chalk. But I did not know how to keep moving.

Robert Bly came in. "James asks when these men are going to stop complaining about their fathers. Well, I don't know about you but I don't intend to stop for three or four years yet!" But as he proceeded to read a recent poem it became clear how far he had already traveled:

MY FATHER'S NECK

Your chest, hospital gown
Awry, lookays
Girlish today.
It is your bluish
Reptile neck
That has known weather.
I said to you, 'Are
You ready to die?'

MELTING THE STONE

'I am,' you said,
'It's too boring
Around here.' He has in mind
Some other place
Less boring. 'He's
Not ready to go,'
The Doctor said.
There must have been
A fire that nearly
Blew out, or a large
Soul, inadequately
Feathered, that became
Cold and angered.
Some four-year-old boy
In you, chilled by your
Mother, misprized
By your father, said,

'I will defy, I will
Win anyway, I
Will show them.'
When Alice's well-
Off sister offered to
Take your two boys
During the Depression,
You said it again.

Now by living you speak
Defiant words to death.
This four-year-old
Old man in you does as
He likes: he likes
To stay alive.
Through him you
Get revenge,
Persist, endure,

Overlive, overwhelm,
Get on top.
You gave me
This, and I do
Not refuse it.
It is
In me.

As the poem progressed I had moved back in memory to one of the many hospital rooms in which I had visited my father. This was an early visit; his cancer period. I was about seven, I was lookaying helplessly at his sunken cheeks, warily avoiding the medicated madness in his eyes. Urging him to win his battle, yet fearful of the victory that could only lead to a continual half-life—unstaged, unapplauded, unheeded. I wanted a strong, young, virile father, but this I would never get. Where could I find the blessing in this hopeless scene? How could I turn off the voice that said it was his fault, he just wasn't good enough, didn't love me enough to give me what I needed? I tookay a deep breath and brought myself back to the community of men.

Michael Meade started a fairy tale called "The Six Companions" (in *Grimm Brothers*, "The Six Servants"), in which a young Prince hears of a beautiful Princess living far away with her mother, an evil sorceress who liked collecting the heads of suitors who failed the tasks she set them. The Prince, of course, wants to go and try his luck, but his father, the King, refuses. The Prince falls ill for seven years, until the King allows him to leave home and pursue his desire.

Something appears in a young man's life to set up a necessary conflict with the father. If we got everything we wanted, we would never leave home. Hillman suggested this was an often ignored key ingredient of the father-son relationship. In many of the myths on which our culture is founded, the father is a murderer or betrayer to the son. Jesus on the cross ("Father, why have you forsaken me?"), Abraham with Isaac, and Oedipus all point to this.

The Father has to betray the son, it's in the wiring; it's not in the wiring of the Mother. Smothering is in the wiring of the Mother. You may be angry at the universe because it put betrayal in the Father—and you may be angry at your father because he was not a good Mother!

I was stunned. I had never been able to contemplate anything other than my father's failure to do (my perception of) a father's job. What if betrayal is part of that job? If father does not "fail us," what inspiration do we have to leave his house?

Malidoma P. Somé stood to begin his presentation on tribal initiation. As he spokaye about the trials and tests he had undergone in the Daghara tribe of Western Africa, I thought that in his culture this betrayal did not hit so hard, for the older men knew their responsibility. There the intervention of elders raised other men to a place of equal trust and prominence with the father in the son's psyche. For us, lacking these methods, it was a matter of lowering the father to the level of all the other untrustworthy older male bastards. And we like to think of the third world as poverty stricken.

My heart began to beat faster as Malidoma continued. He spokaye of initiation not as some mystical religious experience, but as practical education, the purpose of which is not to learn an established body of knowledge, but simply to learn about yourself; to find the project which defines the rest of your life.

There it was, so simple and yet so elusive. The ritual trials were the place where the boy would find the spark of inspiration to lead him into manhood and towards his rightful responsibility. Malidoma had not been left to try and figure it out all by himself, nor had he been told what to do by some guru or priest figure. He had been observed as he went through "one of the most painful things I have ever experienced."

The added incentive was survival itself. As he put it, "You either succeed and live, or fail and die." This was the hard fact, though for the Daghara the type of boy who could not succeed would be a danger to the whole tribe if he lived. As modern society is rapidly realizing, males stuck in boyhood will become destructive to their communities, their families, and to themselves. Maybe the deadly potential was a necessary evil—the non-survival of the unfittest.

Malidoma had entered an initiation circle several years later than the usual age (13-17). His father had handed him over to Jesuit priests when he was five, and he had not seen his tribe or family again until age twenty, when he left the seminary. While there he had forgotten his native language. The children were encouraged to do this by having a rotting cow's skull placed around their necks when caught speaking anything other than French. So when he returned, unable to communicate even with his own parents, the elders decided the only solution was to put him through initiation.

He told us a few of the trials he was allowed to reveal, which would not be appropriate to repeat here. (The interested reader is referred to his recent bookay *Of Water and the Spirit—Ritual, Magic, and Initiation in the Life of an African Shaman.*) Through these, and other far more dangerous tests—some involving journeys to "other worlds"—he learned that:

> Our eyes see only a tiny portion of the visual range that is avail-
> able to us. There are systems of knowledge that create access
> beyond the physical veil. Our sight is made the way it is so that
> we can go through the pain of increasing it. If we were given the
> full range of "sight" from birth we would not have the opportu-
> nity to grow.

Having overcome his greatest fears in order to survive, he became convinced that no one group of people knows better than another group of people—contrary to the Jesuit teachings he had endured for fifteen years. Part of the "life project" he had discovered was to put different systems of knowledge together, and to protect his "traditional education." It still exists in Africa, but is threatened by the will to Westernize that invades most surviving tribes. Africa, he assured us, has far more to offer the world than we could ever imagine. He hoped that some of us would go there and tell them what they have is valuable, before it is irretrievably lost.

It is difficult to explain how, but I knew this man was not bullshitting. He had visited the other realities he had described, survived, undergone twelve years of Western education (emerged with three MAs and two Ph.Ds), and was endeavoring to bridge the gap between these two worlds.

I had been transported into a new realm of possibilities. My spine was tingling with excitement at the tales of his trials, my mind mourning that there was no conceivable equivalent in my culture. Nowhere in Western civilization could anyone be willingly placed in the kind of psychic danger necessary in tribal initiation. The inner-city gang is the modern youth's bastardized version, with no elders and no meaning, only drugs and destruction. The Scout troop is a sanitized, socialized version. The African model could only be appropriate for someone born and bred in that culture anyway. Was it possible to develop a new model, suitable for the Western mind? And if so, where on earth could we start? That afternoon I discovered a small clue.

The Lion Clan gathered in the main meeting hall for two and a half hours of drumming. I was convinced that I would single-handedly prove correct the old adage that "white men have no rhythm," but I was handed a drum and given a simple beat to start with. I picked it up with only slight difficulty, and it became easier still after the next ten minutes of repetition. By this time I was thinking, "Fine, I've got this one now—we can move on." But we didn't. We kept on—and on. For two and a half hours. Boom . . . pad dum—boom . . . pad dum dum. The beat etched itself into my brain waves, into my heartbeat, until it drove out all other thoughts, all other feelings, and became epic in size.

I watched my hands, fascinated that they could now take over without conscious instruction. Then, of course, I would get cocky, lookay away and lose the beat completely. I would start again, wind up more quickly this time, get in the groove of the pulse that pounded inexorably through the room. Then, after another indeterminate period of time, the beat seemed to segue into slow motion:

Booooooom . . . paaad duuuuum—

booooooom . . . paaad duuuuum duuuuum.

Knowing that the tempo had, in reality, remained constant, my mind would snap me back to "real time," just to prove it could, while some other part of me deeply resented this interruption of my trance-like state. And so it went on, my wrists passing through pain barriers which, through focusing back on the beat, could be dissolved.

Later on still, I felt a question forming in my brain: "Why am I here in this place?" No sooner had I silently sounded the words than a reply echoed back from the depths: "To receive a gift." It was unexpected, a weird non-answer that left me searching for more information. But the conscious impatient effort intruded on the rhythm, and once more I was out of synch.

By the time we finished my head was buzzing with unfamiliar though not uncomfortable energy. My hands were simply numb— as I walked outside they settled into a vibrant ache, replete with the power of the drum. Through the communal investment in ritual activity, we had become open to a deeper, different type of thinking. For me it was more intuitive, less intellectual. And, since the whole camp had become our ritual space for the week, I would not have to completely close up the lower level. A barrier had been breached. It left me feeling vaguely vulnerable, though not in danger.

The heat was turned up in "community time," when Jo Walker relayed a request that the black men meet by themselves. The friction it caused was immediate. I felt suddenly, but for no logical reason, intimidated. An Indian man rose to say that if the black and white groups split he would feel "cut in two." Others pointed out how long it had taken to get us together, why separate now?

Abati rose to defend his request. "There is an ancient fear white men have that whenever black men get together, it has to do with white men. This meeting would have nothing to do with white folks . . . It wouldn't be a separation, because we are already separated. I came here to interact with the brothers—I know all the white men I need to know—I know everything about you . . ."

A white man loudly interrupted him, "No, you don't—we don't even know ourselves!"

The crossfire quickened. Questions of trust, safe space, and prejudice mingled with personal stories that sent arrows of emotion racing across the room. From the hundreds of heartfelt statements heard that night, what follows is a verbal collage of those I will never forget. To preserve the spirit of trust the evening created, anonymity is given to those men who were not named teachers for the event.

"Black men don't have to ask permission of anyone to do anything—if you want to meet, go ahead and meet . . . The fact that you think you have to ask is part of the problem." (Haki)

"We are used to being seen as a negative—white vs. nonwhite. I want to change the terms. Men of Color and Men of No Color—think of yourselves in the negative for a while."

"As a child I was abused, ritually, by a group of men in the mountains. This is the first time I've been back in the mountains with a group of men since it happened. It's going okayay . . . but I know that the first thing I have to do is find safety—or I keep trying to protect myself. If some men here need to get together to feel safe, they should be allowed to do it."

"We have only been here a day and we are already shaken up. We see the possibilities that have been opened up. We are anxious to see that there is a tomorrow for this present, because we want to make a difference. We are working on the new community we are trying so hard to build—where there is no color—only humans; men lookaying at each other." (Malidoma)

"We are hiding something here—and that is that white men also need to feel safe in relation to black men. When I saw (Haki's) T-shirt, 'By any means necessary . . .' I found it frightening, because where I live in New York my girlfriend has been threatened with rape and I have been threatened with murder. So if you're going to come at me with 'any means necessary,' then I gotta defend myself with 'any means necessary.' We also need to feel safe."

"I came here yesterday and saw on the registration list another man who shares my last name. I talked to him and we figured out that our families arrived in the same city at the same time. They were probably on the same slave ship and may have been part of the same family."

"I understand the concern some of the white folk have. I would be worried if I saw all the white men going down the hill some-where to meet. I'd run to the brothers and say, 'There's some shit going down here!' We have to acknowledge that we are former enemies, and we need to work on trust—slowly."

"I am a Native American—there is a story about my tribe's knowledge. When the white man came, the medicine men knew that they would have to hide their knowledge, but they didn't know where to put it—everywhere they thought of they figured the white man would find it—until one medicine man had an idea, 'Put it in the white man's heart; he'll never think of lookaying there.'"

"Don't expect me to believe in equality; because when guys like me cross the street—guys like you lock your car door . . ."

"And don't you tell me that when I hear footsteps behind me, that it's guilt that makes me scared. Fuck that shit!"

"You, as European Americans, have to accept that when you come into this room, you come in with four thousand years of power behind you. We are not going to get very far unless we are willing to listen to this anger and this rage. It is genuine. You can hear it and you can feel it. Our job now is to remain in the room, to neither turn away nor resort to violence." (Michael)

"I have been in this black skin for seventy-four years—and all my life I didn't want justice . . . I wanted *revenge*. I have been in AA and stayed dry now for thirty-three years. And I know the pain of being loved and cared for by people you hate intensely."

MELTING THE STONE

I stared into the kind, rugged face of this old man; filled with a sympathy I would never communicate. He wanted to express the hate he had lived with for so long, and the last thing he needed was another white bastard telling him how sorry they felt.

After two hours at this pitch, I felt as if someone had cut into my chest, pulled my heart out and used it as a trampoline. Michael Meade stood to end the evening with a deep breathing exercise that restored a sense of external reason—but inside I was still drunk with emotion as I wended my way along the stony path to Cabin 10 and bed.

Haki Madhubuti upped the ante considerably the next morning with a blistering report on black history in the West. The source of the presentation was his bookay *Black Men—Obsolete, Single, Dangerous?*:

> I don't hate anyone—but I dislike a lot of people. Hate consumes and does not allow us to do anything else. Individually I don't fear anyone; collectively I do fear white men, because of the amount of destruction they have caused.
>
> One half of the men here are my brothers; the other half are potential friends—who may end up being brothers, because connections cross boundaries. I can't put evil on you, because you are here. We have to listen and hear each other—we don't need to travel long distances to shout at each other.
>
> I am here because this is history making—we're starting at a new level of history. [After this conference] if I'm in a room with a thousand white men and one of you is there—I will feel less threatened . . . You paid good money to come and you knew black men were going to be here, so I have to respect that—if nothing else.

He listed the appalling Statistics facing modern black men in America. One in three is involved in the criminal justice system; most between the ages of 16-29, "the warrior years." It costs more to keep a black man in prison per year than it does to put him through university. There are currently more black men in prisons than in universities.

He spokaye of the importance of culture—of how it can lead to a shared understanding—of it being the "medium through which meaning is passed down generations." But black men have been separated from their soil, their soul, and their relatives. They have been "denatured" from their own culture:

"You take an elephant out of Africa. You take that elephant to the United States. You put that elephant in a circus and you make that elephant jump through hoops. But in Africa elephants don't jump through hoops." ". . . I tell my students, 'If you want to be a criminal, don't steal purses, get a Law degree!'" ". . . We don't know where we want to go, because we don't know where we have been, and we don't know where we are now . . . We are programmed to rejection before we can see that rejection." ". . . I'm not in awe of white people, because if I had four million slaves, I could build a country too."

His words sliced through the room. It was hard to contemplate the legacy of death and destruction that my race had caused his race. Was the chasm too wide to be bridged? I began to feel a little sick in my stomach. As Abati had seemed to suggest, was this even the time for bridge building? Or were the wounds still too raw?

James Hillman came forward, not to offer the hoped for panacea, but to point out how the wounding potential is built into the very language of color. The *Oxford English Dictionary* seemed as good a place as any to start:

> **white** Morally or spiritually pure or stainless; spotless, innocent. Free from malignity or evil intent; innocent, harmless especially as opposed to something characterized as black. Highly prized, precious, dear, beloved.

> **white man** "A man of honorable character such as one associates with a European" (as distinct from a negro) 1883.

141

black Absorbing all light. Characterized by the absence of light. Soiled, dirty. Having dark purposes, malignant, deadly, baneful, disastrous, sinister (1583). Foul, iniquitous, atrocious (1581). Dismal, gloomy, sad (1659). Clouded with anger, threatening, boding ill. Indicating disgrace, censure.

By the time the labels of black and white were attached to different races, they already carried this thought-association baggage, and enhanced racist attitudes. Haki Madhubuti's suggestion that the racial tag be "African-American" rather than "Black" was beginning to make sense.

In order to remain itself, white (the color) has to practice exclusion; when mixed with any other color, it stops being "white." So black, as an opposite, has to be excluded. It becomes "other." In the Christian tradition what is "other" (than itself) is unchristian, impure, and opposed to good. It becomes "evil."

Later on, science added to the linguistic boot. Newton and Keppler, with their development of optics, reduced the visible spectrum of light to that which exists in white, refracted through a prism. White became the "supreme color," while black was defined as a non-color, "the absence of light." Philosophers soon joined in the fun, deciding they were moving into the "Age of Enlightenment." And depth psychology defined darkness as "the unconscious," symbolized specifically by dreams of Africa and "primitive" peoples.

The exclusion of black was complete. Linguistically and religiously defined as the "absence of good," optically defined as the "absence of light," philosophically defined as "without the light of reason," and psychologically defined as the "absence of consciousness."

Hillman said, "In social history, this equation promotes missions and colonization and suggests blacks are savage and stupid." This mentality is based in the language that we use every day. Hillman proposed that we give up such oppositional thinking and move beyond black and white. "For we can't get out of our skins, but we can go out of our minds."

As he finished, I thought my brain would overload from trying to accommodate all the information it had received. Instead, an image loomed in front of my inner vision; a white finger rubbing a black skin. The context was unclear. I struggled to bring it into sharper focus but I had let it go, for the moment.

After lunch the Lion Clan met at one end of the camp in a large indoor-sports pavilion. I lookayed around the huge room with its steel roof and basketball courts, and decided that after the intense cramming of the morning, anything we did here would be an anti-climax. I couldn't have been more wrong.

An assistant teacher led us in a theater-type trust exercise in small groups; each man was gently passed around a circle with his eyes closed, and not dropped. Now we were told to choose a man to go in the middle, whose task would be to get out of the circle, while the rest of us had to keep him in.

Somebody called out Jackie's name, and he was soon surrounded by the group. I thought it would be fun. He didn't. He stood stock still in the middle of the circle for what seemed like an age, then simply said, "I don't want to do this." But blood had been smelt, the pack already formed and we would not let him withdraw. Encouraged to "have a go" from within and without the ring of men, he finally moved, tentatively pushing his shoulder against a couple of linked arms. The circle swelled around its own, closed ranks, cut off the escape. Jackie moved to the other side—the same thing happened. He changed directions, moving faster now, caught in the game.

I felt a pang of sympathy, urged him towards me—I would let him out—but by now he saw no friends there, only a mass of men standing against him. He dropped down, tried to hurl himself between the rapidly moving legs—but the circle sensed his intention, convulsed again and four strong legs moved into the inviting gap. Jackie couldn't stop, or rather was stopped, painfully, by knees impacting his rib cage. He winced, retreated, got up, kept moving—but to no avail, we kept him in.

Eventually he was allowed to stop—by now holding his side slightly—as it was explained that the first part of the exercise should prove impossible for one man. We would now have two men in the middle, and teamwork would improve their chances. I lookayed across at Jackie's pained expression. He had not only been physically injured, but "set up" as well. I wondered what was going through his mind. It was a while before he felt able to tell me.

I had come to this place in a state of childhood fear, and the first days were like starting at my new working-class Scottish school in the late fifties—blanketed with suppressed terror about maniacal, deeply unpredictable characters who just might turn their attention to *me* . . .

When I felt the teacher's hand on my back, pushing me into that ring of men—I went straight into the nightmare of playground bullying I had endured as a child. I immediately hated these bastards and their fucking game. Far too much of this shit as a child had slowly but surely turned me into a highly dangerous person, for a while. I momentarily considered pokaying out a couple of eyes—no, Michael had said no violence—I might not get any supper, or worse. So this bunch of dozy middle-class assholes pushed me around, brokaye my ribs and generally had a good time while I died inside.

Suddenly it was over. But that's how it is in men's work—when the big test comes you are almost always on your own, like a city pigeon with a brokayen wing. Some men want, need, or get comfort when the loneliness hits—I got three brokayen ribs and no comfort; but I'm certainly not complaining about it. There were conference activities I could no longer join. It allowed me to be alone in the Virginian mountains, in a sad silence, thinking of the sadness I see in all people's faces; like a still-proud but at-bay ghost community of homeless souls.

Back in the circle, a young Anglo-Jamaican man, Vaughan, and his white friend Rich were whispering in the center. They turned around, eyes gleaming; fit, young, determined. They ran in opposite directions at the linked arms. Now the circle had to stretch at two points simultaneously. It threatened to break—pulling a sixty-year-old man next to me crashing to his knees. I helped him up, aware of a peculiar lack of control in the circle, and concerned for his safety.

I turned back to see Rich and Vaughan coming straight for us—fast. Rich helped Vaughan up into the air, he ended up doing a flip over my left shoulder and landing outside the circle. As he arched up in the air I knew that I could have obeyed orders—I knew that by moving backwards and dragging the older man with me I could have caused Vaughan to land on our linking arms and fall back into the circle. I stayed still—failed my brief—aware that any further commitment to it would be dangerous. The game finished. The circle disintegrated, thwarted, but the gleam of aggression in many eyes, including mine, was unmistakable. It was the first moment of its kind since we had arrived and it felt unbalanced, ugly, and unkind in this setting.

Now the whole clan gathered to perform a "falling leaf" exercise on a volunteer. An African-American man stepped forward. The rest of us tookay hold of him, cradled him in our arms. A gentle hum was started, he was rocked back and forth then slowly raised above our heads on the fingertips of sixty hands. He lay there, swayed gently for several moments before being lowered into our male cradle, swayed some more and ever so slowly lowered to the ground.

He stayed silent for some time, then began shaking. He gradually became enfolded in large racking sobs that shookay his frame. We stayed sitting around him, supportive but not intrusive. He began to speak; of childhood pain, of prejudice, separation, and confusion; of a growing certainty that he had been diverted from his purpose; of a recent acceptance of a new role, and of coming here to gather strength for it. I felt our clan pouring concentrated male energy into the depth of his being; giving, without thought of receiving. He lay in our midst, accepting this soul food. Slowly the tension eased off his face. Eventually he sat up and smiled, then lookayed slowly around the circle, silently thanking each man in turn.

I got wearily to my feet and joined the natural movement of drained bodies towards air and refreshment. We had almost made it to the door when a voice called out, "Does anyone else want to go?" Before we could express doubt and fatigue, a small group loudly accepted and pushed a stocky African-American man forward. I realized, with a slight shiver, that this was the man I had described as "built like a brick shithouse."

We moved wearily back to the center of the hall, and began to repeat the exercise. This time the emotional release started sooner. This man was trembling as we lifted him up into the air. As he swayed above us his tears flowed freely down. I was standing just behind his head, one hand touching his crown. I felt tears of shame spring to my eyes. Why had I feared this man?

I lookayed up to gaze at the closely cropped ebony head and saw a large tear run down his face. I watched, with guilty fascination, as it gathered weight at the edge of his cheek before falling down. I followed its path, saw it strike the temple of a white man standing in front of me. This man, too, had tears in his eyes. One now welled out to drift down his face. The tear from above, determined to catch it, chased down the cheek, until the tears met on the white chin, hesitated for a second, before joining forces, doubling in size and plummeting down—onto my bare foot. I felt blessed as if by holy water. We were creating magic, sharing tears in ritual space, starting to bridge the chasm we had seen this morning.

Tears streamed down my face as we lowered our friend to the ground. He started telling his story—early tales of rejection, abandonment, fatherlessness; everyone he loved or liked or needed had left him. I felt a deep connection with him, as if I had known him forever, as if I knew what he was going to say.

146

More men were crying now, moans of recognition swelling the emotional tide. Vaughan was sitting in front of me, sobbing as he held a hand on the prone man's chest. But unlike the others he did not stay sobbing for long; his noises rapidly escalated into howls of uncontrolled anguish. His body started trembling violently, convulsing as his cries continued unabated. I lookayed around, worried, seeking help from the assistant teacher, still nominally in charge. He indicated that we should split into two groups, half moving away with Vaughan while the other half stayed with our first charge. Being close to Vaughan I moved away with him, all too conscious that the man I was leaving was speaking of abandonment.

The new group lifted Vaughan off the ground into the cradle position, while his cries echoed round the hall, becoming more guttural by the second. He struggled violently in our grasp, trying to break free. Rich lent over him, pressed his head to Vaughan's chest, and gripped tightly, trying to still his friend's convulsions. Suddenly blood appeared on Vaughan's chest—for an awful moment I thought he had somehow stabbed himself—until I saw blood streaming from Rich's nose. Another instruction and Rich was dragged away, screaming that he had to be with Vaughan.

We were now split into three groups. I wondered if we could hold it. What would we do if more men were infected, set off? It began to feel dangerous, control slipping out of our hands, giving sway to untrammeled emotion.

Vaughan increased his struggle, lashing out with no thought for our or his safety, while the guttural sounds had become a strange foreign language. There was no way to calm him. We put him down and stood back watching warily. He stood up unsteadily, as if drunk. His eyes were white, the pupils had all but disappeared, his nostrils flaring, as he proceeded to yell at us in his new tongue.

He was either in the midst of some psychotic breakdown or possessed. I didn't know which I would rather it was. He set off, walking fast and erratically in large circles, snorting aggressively at any one he came close to, while the strange monologue continued. I had a weird sensation in my chest. Just panic? Or did it herald the beginning of something else? I had been holding Vaughan—had "it" got into me too?

We stood around for several minutes, unsure, regaining our breath and some semblance of composure. The other two prone men had calmed down now, the tension released from their circles. Ours had split up and we continued to watch Vaughan's perambulations. He did not stop, so we gathered uneasily in a final circle to close the afternoon—but it didn't feel closed to me.

We were sent off for tea, but in my anxiety I hung around to see what would happen. A few men carefully walked Vaughan to his cabin while another fetched Malidoma Somé. I sat under a nearby tree and waited. I was trembling, lightheaded. Part of me wanted to head off into the woods and release my own emotions; another part of me knew it was too dangerous alone. Logic and fear won. I willed myself to settle down. But I could not yet tear my mind away from the experience. I had stared briefly into the unknown—and needed some explanation. I was quietly determined to continue this kind of ritual work in England, but this had shaken me up. If I had yearned for some kind of danger in our initiatory trials this week, I had just got it.

After an age Malidoma emerged from the cabin. I went over quickly and told him my involvement and concern. He said that Vaughan had been through "a spiritual emergency," that he had had to do some work with his tribal medicine bag, and that Vaughan should be okayay with rest and quiet.

It would be two years before I met Vaughan again and asked him about that afternoon. It had taken him the better part of those two years to work it out for himself:

I had had a strong gut feeling that I had to come to this conference. When I arrived I felt totally in control. I laughed when Michael talked about saving your breakdown for a week. I thought that I was on my own inner journey, which would end on a mountain top with some wonderful experience. So when all this started my first thought was, 'What the hell's going on? This isn't supposed to happen now and it isn't supposed to happen like this!'

I had been in some kind of initiation process of my own for about a year, since leaving college. That space every young man goes through, asking the big three questions, 'What am I doing with my life? Why am I here? What am I supposed to do?' But I was probably doing it more intensely than most. Constantly reading, constantly meditating and spacing out. I didn't talk about it to anyone. I kept it all locked up.

So I felt very vulnerable when I started to cry. I just wanted to be there for this other guy. I didn't want to be a burden to anyone. But I was tapping into all my locked-up pain and suddenly I couldn't contain it. Then it felt as though I was tapping in to this other guy's pain, and I couldn't contain that, and then the pain of the whole group. I felt such pain, as if I'd become the anchor for everyone there, and I couldn't stop it. It was really frightening.

Throughout the experience there were two 'me's' —one going through it and one watching. When I started to freak out and pull my hair out, the watcher was thinking, 'Why is this happening to me?' Even when I started walking round and speaking like that, the watcher was thinking (in English), 'Am I going to be speaking like this for the rest of my life?' I didn't have a choice—it was 'go this way—or die.'

But if I hadn't handled it the way I did I think I could have gone mad. Immediately after I was scared shitless. I asked for Malidoma. He told me that I had gone briefly into another reality and there was a danger that I could disappear into that other world at any moment. I had to keep thinking positive thoughts or something could happen again.

I was like a baby going out into the world, I couldn't speak properly for the next few days—only brokayen English. It felt like a kind of rebirth.

And when I left the conference the direction that I'd had before was gone. I couldn't go back and it's taken me two years to fully deal with it. But now I see how it opened me up to be an antenna for the pain of others. I work with children now. That experience released something inside of me that can be sensitive to their hurts.

I was able to stop seeing myself in a role and start seeing myself as a person. I see myself now, not as a black person, but as someone who has black skin; not as a musician, but as someone who plays music; not as a counselor but as someone who counsels.

Listening to Vaughan talk, it struck me that he had, indeed, undergone a kind of initiation. He had risked a death and been reborn as someone unattached to previous perceptions of himself and able, eventually, to see himself as a human being—complete with an active, emotional body.

Lookaying back on the event as I write, Vaughan's episode was a turning point. As if he really had become an anchor for the group. Before that afternoon the primary emotion was anger. After it, other feelings arose and everyone seemed to be more willing to listen. If he had somehow attracted the combined rage of these hundred men, it's not surprising it tookay him two years to recover. He was lucky to be alive.

The following "community time" began with a European-American man from the south speaking of growing up in a racist household. "As a child I was taught that the way I could right the world would be to restore slavery . . .", cries of "tough job!" mixed with laughter from the floor. Next up was a son of southern gentry whose ancestors had owned slaves. His father and brother were racist to this day, and his sense of shame had forced him to leave home—causing a massive loss of identity. As he sadly listed memories of racism towards maids and laborers, some other men began gently weeping.

A third white man stood, obviously affected by what had gone before. He stayed standing, silently, until he summoned the courage to make his confession. In the orphanage where he grew up, he and some friends had chased a new black kid out of the house and down the street, and then built a cross in the garden, wrapped the boy's clothes around it and set it alight. . . . Hisses of outrage sounded through the room. The speaker lookayed around nervously; but if he was asking for forgiveness, he did not receive it. The applause as he sat was for his honesty.

Now an African-American spokaye, "I'm having a problem with a kind of lie that seems to be allowed here. . . . We've talked about growing up with the line that 'a nigger ain't shit,' but below a nigger is a faggot. And no one is addressing that. We need to see what is soft that we're trying to protect and see what is secret that we are trying not to say—and let it go. Because that is the only way we are going to get together."

A white man stood to announce himself as "a gay warrior." He accused this conference of being more homophobic than any other he had attended. He had brought his own question to Buffalo Gap, "Is this men's work or just straight men's work?"

An African-American jumped in, "If I see men kissing each other on the lips—I want to punch them on the lips. It is anti-family. I have sons, and if I found out that their teachers were gay, I would take them out of school."

Others rose to argue against his prejudice, until Malidoma spokaye. In his tribe gay people were the gatekeepers to the spiritual world. Men who were fathers and responsible for families would not have the energy or the insight for this. Gay men were called "Dapo," meaning "man-woman." They were valued because they could see into two worlds and help hold the society together. During his initiation he had sought comfort through human touch to gain courage to continue: "Men's relationships can go a long way before they get sexual. There is much to admire in people whose sexuality seems strange. So explore that—then if and when you are 'proposed to' you can talk about what you like and dislike."

A white man stood to speak with dignity and strength: "If any-one here has reason to be afraid of touch it is me. As a small child I was taken into a form of slavery. I was assaulted. I was impris-oned. My dignity was taken away, and I was emasculated. The first man who held me, anally raped me. I had a lot of rage and grief about that. But that was yesterday. I'm a powerful man now, and I have the power to say 'yes' when I mean 'yes,' and 'no' when I mean 'no.' I want you to ask me before you touch me—but I invite safe touch, and I hope we can all do that."

Another emotional battering. As the evening drew to a close I realized how important the listening was. I was hearing realities of masculine experience that went far beyond racism and sexism. The raw energy involved was unbelievable. The more passion and preju-dice that were thrown into the pot, the deeper and stronger the pot became. Despite the exhaustion it was hard to go to sleep, images and words from the day swirled inside my head.

At breakfast I was sitting with my small group when Haki Madhubuti came over and sat with us. He ate in silence for a few minutes while we spokaye of the previous evening's statements. Then he lookayed up and said, simply, "I never knew white men had so much pain." For a moment I was shocked. But then I re-called the title of one of his bookays, *Enemies: The Clash of Races*. That this intellectual, "by any means necessary," African warrior had been moved by members of the "enemy" race was testimony to the true power of the event.

I lookayed into his face, then turned away, embarrassed at the emotion I felt. Another image floated in front of my eyes, another black face. It was chiseled, noble, strong, strangely familiar. The mists of memory cleared. It was my father as Othello. I was shocked—this was my earliest conscious memory of him, the only one that pre-dated illness. I saw within it the kind of strength I had sought for so long. A gift I had been searching for that had been waiting in my own bloodline.

I spent most of the day in a kind of reverie, wondering how I had dismissed my father's amazing ability to fight death as weakness. And realizing too that it was probably because he had rarely been home when he was strong. He stayed at home only when he was too ill to work.

As we entered "community time" we were reminded that this was the last chance for personal statements, and those who had not yet spokayen were encouraged to do so. My heart began to pound. I did want to speak. While I waited for inspiration, Abati stood up and invited everyone interested to a late-night meeting to demonstrate a "Recovery from the Consequences of Slavery" program. He added that he was starting to get sad about leaving the conference. He would miss us. Someone shouted, "Even the white men?" He smiled and said, "Yes—I can't believe it!" to much applause.

I was sitting in front of him and tookay this as my cue. I rose, still trying to figure out how to focus my thoughts, and stated my full name. Before I could continue Abati brokaye in, "Any relation?" I stopped and hesitated. This was the point when I normally withdrew, feeling diminished—but in this place I tookay up the challenge. "Yes, I am Laurence Olivier's son—and I've never said that in public before . . ." A few men started applauding. Abati shouted, "Say it again!" I smiled, caught between laughter, tears, and embarrassment—and said it again, a little louder. Abati wouldn't let up, "One more time!" I lookayed him in the eyes, he was grinning broadly. I grinned back, aware of an unbottling of tension stored up for years—ever since I became aware my father was a famous man. "I am the son of Laurence Olivier." It was stronger still, an acceptance I had been running from all my life.

I tookay a deep breath and carried on, saying that I must be the only white man present whose first memory of his father was as a black man. My first memory of a real black person was from the same time, while Dad was playing Othello. One day, after a performance, while waiting for Dad to shower off the black boot polish he used as make-up, my sister and I saw a black woman come in the stage door with a pram. Tamsin had gone over to lookay at the baby, then carefully licked her finger and tried to wipe the color off the baby's arm, as she had seen Dad doing.

153

MELTING THE STONE

This was another memory that had returned to me this week and one which seemed symbolic of the work here. We were trying to wipe off the color, wipe away prejudice, and see a common humanity. A veil had lifted for me when a black man I imagined a threat became a man trying to cope with his pain, someone not unlike myself. As a white man I may have to see the "whiteness" under the black skin before I recognize the "same"; a black man may have to see the "blackness" under the white skin to recognize shared experience.

When we just lookay at the surface, we can only see two dimensions, like a caricature—a stereotype—and can maintain prejudice. But when we add depth to the image and see another dimension, the stereotype fades, to reveal the three-dimensional human being. The understanding that comes with seeing the whole person destroys pre-judged attitudes.

During our time together here, the sharing of pain and the expression of anger and grief had opened the doors of our vision to accommodate a new, deeper perception of each other. We had been allowed to see under each other's skin and even, at moments, to feel we had been in other skins. It had been a true lesson in how to fight prejudice.

The black image of my father held a kingly strength I needed to find. And it had been a gift from these black men. At the age of five I had seen it in my father, but soon after he became ill, and I had not seen it again until this week—when my soul had been stirred by the black kings I had met here.

Abati stood up and began to clap. Old feelings of unworthiness threatened to overwhelm me. Other men joined him and I was in a battle of inner voices—old ones saying, "It's got nothing to do with you—it's all because of your father,"—newer ones telling them to "Fuck off—I have things to say and do in my own right." It wasn't easy but I held my ground. I sat down, flushed, stretched between poles of elation and emptiness. I sat in this state all evening. Glowing. I went to bed proud of my heritage for the first time in a long, long while.

Time had slowed down all week—if someone had said we had been in the camp for a month it would not have surprised me—but now, almost imperceptibly, it began to speed up. Our last full day mixed presentations with preparations for "Carnivale"—a celebration meal, toasts, drumming, and dancing. As dinner ended, the toasting began. Men spokaye words of praise to others. The depth of feeling and gratitude that swept through the room over the next hour was stunning. Often before these men had spokayen of themselves, of failures, problems, and pain—now they spokaye generously of others, of the men who had impressed them and of the resolutions they would take away with them. "Let's make a deal. When we think that we see each other in the street—come running—and let's shock the hell out of everyone that we're with!"

If, on that first night, we had called on people or spirits who had been with us in the past, now, on the last night, we were naming those here whose spirits would remain with us in the future. It was a mutual acknowledgment. The men at the top table had been instigators, catalysts, and containers for the event; but the living, pounding heartbeat had been supplied by all of us, and we would not forget it.

We moved over to the dance floor to watch James Hillman perform a tap dance accompanied by Vaughan. The sight of this gracefully aging white man, elegantly tapping away to the harsh and urgent beauty of the young black man's saxophone, was extraordinary. Vaughan, who could still hardly speak, was communicating through music, while Hillman's brilliant mind was now focused in his floating feet. The pair of them created one more magical image for us to take away.

As they finished, a hundred men cheered and swarmed onto the floor. We divided ourselves into drummers and dancers, and continued for as long as we could stand. Not having brought a drum, and feeling deeply inferior rhythmically to the crescendo of sound being pounded out on a wall of instruments, I quickly decided I was a dancer—for tonight anyway.

MELTING THE STONE

Lines of men swayed across the floor, some daubed with body paint, adding a distinctly tribal feel to the controlled frenzy. On and on we went, reveling in this creative expression of our masculinity, not concerned with lookays or performance, only celebration. Smells normally quickly extinguished in locker rooms hung over the floor in sour-sweet pungent clouds. It was intoxicating, and I was swept up in the dazzling energy on display.

Later on, two men brought in a broom handle for limbo dancing. After two bruising failures I thought it was time to show off something I could do, so I raised the broom to shoulder height for a diving roll that I hadn't practiced for eight years. Somewhere in my mind I must have known I was not going to get out of this one unscathed, but I didn't care.

I backed away, lookayed at the stick, ran up and sailed over. I just about cleared the stick, and I was busy congratulating myself on this when I lookayed down and realized that I couldn't see the floor. There was just an indefinable darkness, brokayen only by the vague shapes of surrounding legs. There was no way to judge distance, no way to break my fall accurately—I extended an arm, hoping to roll over it and neatly onto my back—no such luck. I was plummeting down, felt the arm connect but not roll. It crumpled, helpless, and I landed heavily on my head and left shoulder. There was a flash of pain and a lot of stars. I felt briefly humiliated, but more important, in that moment, was not to show weakness, not to express pain. I quickly picked myself up, assured the worried broom handlers that I was okay and danced as fast as my aching head would allow.

However boyish the episode may seem in the cold light of day, it was a last barrier for me to break through that week. All my life I had shied away, giving in to school yard bullies, enduring any humiliation rather than risk physical pain. I had always felt a coward as a result. In this impulsive, exuberant, and foolish moment, I had exorcised a ghost. Calling perhaps on the courage I had found in Othello's face, I had dived into the father's house, towards certain pain, knowing that if I was not prepared to risk pain, rejection, and failure, I would never be fully engaged in life.

I decided to think of the stabbing ache in my shoulder as my "initiatory wound," there to remind me of what I had learned. On the other hand maybe I was just jealous of Jackie's brokayen ribs.

The pall of imminent departure mingled with dance hangovers in next morning's early light. Time had speeded up; we had now slowed down. We gathered to close the event, unwinding a huge circle of men, shaking each man's hand as we went. The sense of community was astonishing. As I moved round I was genuinely sad I would not be seeing these men again—even though I was not aware of their existence a mere six days before. We had shared intimate secrets, things some of our closest friends would never know. It was not a naive wish that we would all stay close friends—but a recognition of mutual humanity—a rare connection, that once made cannot be unmade.

The car ride back to Washington DC was like watching a silent movie. Nothing seemed real—the cars were props, the people in them extras. No one spokaye much. There was nothing more to say. We sat with our own reflections, heavy with the weight of the week.

Back at our hotel, Jackie and I headed resolutely for the bar, where an array of multicolored cocktails appeared to compensate for our dry week. Needless to say, we were well out of mythic space three hours later, when Robert Bly called to say our meeting, planned for the next day, would have to take place now. We made a quick dash for the swimming pool, managed to avoid drowning and/or throwing up, showered, coffeed, dressed and taxied over to Robert and Michael's hotel—walking with some care over the thick carpet from the door of the suite to the proffered chairs.

The meeting was about their upcoming event in England in September, and we sorted out the practical considerations first. I asked if we could try and set up some of the ritual elements that had proven so effective over the past week, and they agreed. Talk turned to Buffalo Gap. They, too, felt it had been a staggering event with vital implications for the future of men's work. Just what these were

MELTING THE STONE

we would all have to wait and see. But already it seemed that Henry Wadsworth Longfellow had been proved crucially right:

> If we could read the secret history of our enemies, we should find in each man's life sorrow and suffering enough to disarm all hostility.

Chapter Eight

In the Father's House

With hindsight, that week in Buffalo Gap was another turning point. Not because I was suddenly possessed of strength I previously lacked, but because the image of paternal strength was a beacon. I had finally found the inspiration to cross the threshold of the father's house. But as soon as I stepped in I saw how old the door was, how dirty the walls were, how gloomy the rooms were within. As my eyes gradually adjusted to this new half-light, I started to sort through the contents. There I found, among assorted junk, several dangerous traps and a few hidden treasures.

At the first men's group meeting after our return Jackie and I attempted to convey as much of our recent trip as possible. Some of the energy we had felt there must have been transmitted, as by the end of the meeting the group agreed to start regular drumming, invite new men to join, pursue ritual activities, move from Jackie's sitting room to a more neutral space and start a rotating leadership. Maintaining my role as the pushy director, I quickly got myself chosen as the first leader.

It was actually quite nerve racking. For all my gung-ho enthusi-
asm, attempting to lead this small group of men into new territory,
without a map, would not be easy. And though I racked my brain
for the next week, a sensible idea refused to emerge. In the end I
decided to halve the risk and adapt a favorite theater rehearsal tech-
nique for the purpose.

So, at the next meeting, we did some relaxation exercises, and
ended up lying on the floor. Then I asked the men to close their
eyes and imagine a corridor in front of them. When they "saw"
this they could allow an image of their father to appear at the end
of it. Then allow this figure to walk down the corridor towards
them. Look at him. Observe how he walks, how his arms swing,
how he holds his head. Let him stop to stand directly in front of
them. Look at his features. See which, if any, they had inherited.
Then, when they were ready, slowly let this figure move into their
bodies. Bearing my recent experience with Vaughan firmly in mind,
I pointed out that this was *not* the father's spirit, and we were not
being possessed by the father in any way. It was simply an acting
exercise in which we might feel what we had inherited from the
father. We would be acting an image. When this image had entered
our body, we should "try it out," get up and walk around. Try and
move as the father's image moved, and see what it felt like.

Having only done this exercise with actors imagining fictional
characters, I did not really know what to expect. But soon I witnessed an eerie sight. These men, whose own movement patterns I
knew, now emphasized some familiar gestures, while incorporat-
ing others I had not seen, as they acted their father.

When they had all started, I sat down, relaxed, and waited for
my father's image. But as a figure appeared at the end of the corridor I flinched. This was not the strong man who could play Othello
twice a day; it was the weak old man, close to death. I tried to
change his shape, banish him and summon the other—but he would
not go, lurking in my mind's eye, until I unwillingly accepted him.
He walked towards me with characteristic painful slowness; ach-

ing joints and hands curled with cramp. Could I let this baleful old man into my body? It was my exercise—I had to.

I bowed to the inevitable, sensing the weight of his gravity-bent spine as it moved into mine, followed by the operation-scarred body, tense in expectancy of further injury. Beady gray eyes forced mine into sharper focus, ever watchful for surprising obstacles. I ambled around the room, oblivious now to the other men, consumed in my own father. I found myself resenting the age, and the subsequent fall from public greatness to private incapacity. I tried to move forcefully, powerfully, as I had seen him try to do so often, the frame barely containing the will, but unable, finally, to do its bidding. I sat, carefully but not gracefully, on a sofa, raising the thrombosis-ridden leg up to ease its pain. I watched an imagined door, ready to look daggers at any younger, thoughtless passers-by who would leave it open and abandon me to numbing draughts.

My physical discomfort was intense but the emotional reality I was being sucked towards seemed worse. I excused myself by thinking the others must have had enough. I shut my eyes, mentally disengaged the image and watched it shuffling awkwardly away from me, back down the corridor to infinity. He turned and waved—slowly—then he was gone.

I pulled the others out of it, and we talked through the experience. Most had found it valuable. "I never realized I had my father's hands."—"I want to do it again, for longer . . ."—"I could feel how defensive he is, all the time, never letting anything in . . ." For a couple of men it had been too confrontational. One newcomer was sitting, quiet and pale, in a corner. At the last conference he had spoken of a fearful physical conflict with his father. Now he said the idea of an image of his father entering his body had made him feel physically sick. He knew he had some hard work to do.

As did I. For reasons I could not yet fathom, this weak old father I had seen must be my predominant father image. Maybe even my primary male role model. There was something here that demanded attention.

161

MELTING THE STONE

Over the next few weeks I carefully explored the ramifications of this disturbing image, in my journal, in analysis, and in the men's group. I even tried to put myself back in the image, back in his shoes, bit by painful bit, and sense a little part of his feelings. Of course, on one level it was all in the imagination, all done in the confines of my own head. But it did seem to help, or at least lead to greater understanding.

Part of my discomfort with the "old man" came from the fact that he was someone who was supposed to "have it all"—fame, wealth, family—but seemed unhappy with it. Off the stage, out of the limelight, there was no fire to warm his soul, no inspiration to turn him on. It was as if he had made a Mephistophelian deal early in his life, to be a one-trick pony: "You make me the best in the world at one thing, and I won't care about the rest." When the years of greatness had ravaged his body and rendered him unable to act any more, he could find nothing else to do. And little else to enjoy.

Alice Miller warns that "morality and duty are artificial measures that become necessary when something essential is lacking" (*For Your Own Good*, p. 85). I had tried to run away into "duty" and work. Maybe it was a family trait. After all, both my father's and mother's lives had been geared to serving Theater, and I had been drawn to the same line of service. I had had to choose between accepting or rejecting their "god" as one worthy of worship, or rejecting it while the child felt it was preferred over him. There was no real choice. I had to believe in this god who demands such painful sacrifices—because that made my parents servants of a good cause.

I had carefully traced my "lack" back to often absent, hardworking parents and the disciplines they had imposed to facilitate their work. In which case my father's workaholism may well have had its roots in his upbringing. Maybe he turned to the theater for the adoring eyes he had been denied at home, due to his mother's early death and his father's devotion to the Anglican Church. Maybe the actor was created specifically so the boy/man did not have to feel the pain. A "false self" built for desperate defense that then lost touch with the original reality.

> In my heart of hearts I only know that I am far from sure when I am acting and when I am not or, should I more frankly put it, when I am lying and when I am not.
>
> (*Confessions of an Actor*, p. 24-5)

So acting became an addictive painkiller. And the reason he never really felt happy when he was not working was because he was suffering withdrawal from his fix.

Often while sorting through all this, I had felt angry with him—for staying away when he was well and only wanting me around when he was ill; for, apparently, loving me only when I could help look after him, and for giving me the subconscious message that strong men are absent fathers, only weak men are home. But one night, lying in bed unable to sleep, the anger slowly shifted into a deep melancholy. He had done what he had to do in order to survive—no more, no less, which is an ultimately human gesture. Who was I to blame him if he hadn't ever been able to dismantle the defense?

As if of its own accord, the image of the old man appeared in front of my closed eyes. This time I willed it towards me, urged it to sink into my body. And allowed myself to feel what I had run away from before. I felt his wounds as if they were my own, and knew the awful sadness he had carried his whole life. It was heavy, empty, and helpless. A large weight in the pit of my stomach that threatened to drag me down to unknown depths of sorrow where I would drown, awash in unshed tears. A dark pond of despair that would swallow all affection like a black hole swallows matter.

It was a moment of connection that shook me. I floated within his sphere for as long as I could, then came back to myself, flooded with new respect that he had never shared this burden, and never complained about it. This was the strength in the Othello face: to endure, to survive, to overcome immense pain despite the odds. The paradox was that the one came with the other. The weak man came at the end of the strong man's life, came, perhaps, as a *result* of the strong man's life. I could not take one without the other.

As a teenager I had only seen the frail man. My example of strength had come primarily from my mother, working hard while supervising three children, two households, and an ill husband. I had sought her protection and placed myself in the "soft male" trap where imagined sensitivity becomes an excuse for cowardice. Recent inner work had caused a shift in the balance—and now an unconscious battle began. I had entered the father's house, but the dark side of the Great Mother did not want me to stay there. As Robert Bly points out, we should not blame the personal mother for the archetypal "smothering" potential:

> For Freud has already singled her out, wrongly, for the main responsibility. The whole initiatory tradition, of which Freud knew very little, lays the primary responsibility on men, particularly on the older men and the ritual elders. They are to call the boys away. *When they don't do that, the possessive side of the Great Mother will start its imprisonment, even though the personal mother doesn't want the negative holding to take place.*
>
> (*Iron John*, p. 187—my emphasis)

As with most conflicts, this one started innocuously enough. Shelley and I had planned a holiday in Spain, and one afternoon she asked Joan if she wanted to come and visit while we were over there. I instinctively flinched, sensing it was bad timing, coming just as I was trying to get free of parental shadows. But I didn't say anything. Fear of causing offense, fear of not being a "nice boy," fear of imagined maternal resentment swallowing me up—whatever it was, I stayed silent and sulked.

So the plans were made, Shelley and the kids left and I stayed with Joan at the country cottage. She was organizing a large gathering of friends to commemorate the second anniversary of Larry's

death, at which we would announce the October date for the inter-
ment of his ashes at Westminster Abbey. I was trying to finish some
work. We embarked on a series of minor skirmishes when I felt she
was impinging unfairly on my time to help with her party plans.
And had our first adult shouting match when I refused to give up
my last full work day to paint some old chairs for the occasion. It
was, of course, fairly bloody typical that when I finally found a
voice to stand up to my mother it was to protect work and not time
with my wife and children. The showbiz ethics were still in the
bloodstream.

Off I went to Spain, for a great few days, until I returned to the
airport to pick up my mother. From this moment on I felt under
increasing stress. This was purely internal psychic pressure—Joan
was sweetness and light throughout her stay—but it didn't help.
There was some unfinished business to take care of, and I would
not be allowed to rest easy until it was done. Since I could not figure out what it was, I did very little. I hung around feeling invaded
by some ancient power, reduced from the "all new improved" man
taking care of his family, to a resentful son annoyed at his willingness to drive around in Mother's rented car—rather than walking
by himself.

The holiday teetered towards the brink of disaster. I felt guilty
about my resentment. After all it was nothing that my mother was
doing; it was what I was *not* doing that lay at the root of the tension. But I did not yet know it, couldn't understand it or explain it
to anyone. It felt so unreasonable, so ungrateful, so unsupportive,
not to want my mother around. And yet I could not help it. I tried
to hide it, fairly unsuccessfully, and then tried to blame my wife,
which didn't work. We could only relax and talk about it after Joan
had left.

A week after our return I had a frightening daydream. I saw myself as a failed middle-aged man, living in Los Angeles but financially
dependent on my working wife. I was pretending to be a film director, but I had never directed a film. Somewhere inside I knew that I

was seen as a charity case, only put up with as a curiosity because I was the son of a famous man. But I kept denying it . . .

I snapped out of it with a shudder. It was as if the mists of time had briefly lifted to let me see a possible future. I realized then that if I continued to rely on strong feminine figures for support, this would be the kind of fate that awaited me. All the work I had done so far would count for nothing if I couldn't muster the courage to talk honestly to my mother.

And so, a couple of days later, I found myself standing outside her front door with my finger on the doorbell. I was desperately struggling to remember that I was six feet tall and nearly thirty years old, when the door opened. We greeted each other with somewhat forced bonhomie, and I led the way into the sitting room, my heart pounding so loud I felt sure she would hear it. Fearful questions shot through my brain. What the hell will I say? How will I say it? Can I say it? And how will she take it? Of course, the dreadful anticipation was infinitely worse than the actual event, but that didn't help me then. I sat uneasily and stared doggedly at the coffee table, gathering focus and avoiding the temptation to slip into our usual pattern of work-related discussion.

I started by apologizing for the silly rows we had been having. She said she understood, and knew how exhausting it must be with two young children and working at the same time. Now was the moment. I clutched the arms of my chair for support, and took the plunge.

No, that was not it. Our relationship was the problem. Her eyes opened wide with surprise, and what I interpreted as mild hurt. I quickly looked away. I explained, as best I could, that I felt there was some kind of unhealthy link between us; an invisible umbilical cord that had never been cut. I told her I had come to believe that there was a traditional order of male development—nought to seven with the mother, seven to fourteen with the father, fourteen to twenty-one with the mentor, and thence out into the world. In my case these had been muddled, and often simply missed. As a child I had been looked after by a nanny, while Joan occasionally worked; at seven my father had cancer and had been unavailable; at fourteen he had contracted an awful muscle-wasting disease, I had not wanted to go off with a mentor; at twenty-one, on leaving UCLA, I had allowed my mother to find a job for me in England, where I could help her look after family affairs. As a result of this sequence of events I had never properly separated from the mother. This was not her fault. She had naturally continued to mother me as best she could, but it was not her job to lead me out of the home and into the world. I had recently found the necessary male support to help me in this task. Now I had to break this link and gain some distance. She had to let me go in order that I could eventually return. Then I could be a supportive friend; no longer stuck as a resentful son.

I had single-mindedly continued to address all this to her coffee table. She took it well, on the whole, and—there not being much more that could be said—we parted. My relief at being alive made me extra polite on the way out.

(A few months later, when I thought she may have started to forget this conversation, I photocopied some of *Iron John* and dropped it through her letterbox. Reading six pages on "The Dark Side of the Great Mother" stimulates the memory, and saves on conversation. Maybe every mother should read it, preferably on or before their son's fourteenth birthday.)

Within a week I had a strange dream. I was in a house, which had been built for a horror film. Something huge and snakelike was slithering across the floor towards me. I was terrified. But I didn't run away. I stayed still, wondering what would happen next . . .

The terror reminded me of the childish fear experienced outside my mother's house. And made more sense when I came across the following in *The Hero With a Thousand Faces:*

> a great number of the ritual trials . . . correspond to those that appear automatically in dream the moment the psychoanalyzed patient begins to abandon his infantile fixations. Among the aborigines of Australia, for example, one of the principal features of the ordeal of initiation . . . is the rite of circumcision. When a little boy of the Murngin tribe is about to be circumcised, he is told by his fathers and by the old men, 'The Great Father Snake smells your foreskin; he is calling for it.' The boys . . . become extremely frightened. Usually they take refuge with their mother . . . —Now regard the counterpart from the unconscious. 'One of my patients,' writes Dr. C. G. Jung, 'dreamt that a snake shot out of a cave and bit him in the genital region. This dream occurred at the moment when the patient was convinced of the truth of the analysis and was beginning to free himself from the bonds of his mother-complex."
>
> *(Hero With a Thousand Faces*, p. 10-11)

But the self-congratulation did not last long. It was a bit like playing psychic Space Invaders. As soon as you managed to shoot one monster down, two more appeared behind it. Next into the firing line came a newspaper article about a couple of upcoming books which claimed that my father had had a homosexual relationship with his friend, Danny Kaye.

Since I had never heard the slightest whiff of this rumor before, it was something of a shock. Or more precisely, it sent me into cold-blooded, homophobic paranoia. I went around describing one of the authors as (allegedly), "Having the moral scruples of a necrophiliac rent boy—he likes to screw dead men and get paid for it . . ." But not even passive-aggressive jokes could still my quaking psyche. I was worried.

I swiftly took this subject into analysis, feeling too threatened to broach it in the men's group, and got another jolt. David Kay carefully asked me if I had forgotten what he had told me on our first meeting, that he was distantly related to Danny Kaye. Even to my cynical mind this went beyond coincidence and into the area of "synchronicity." I don't know what the odds would have been against me choosing the one Jungian analyst in London who would prove to be related to a man my father would be accused of having an affair with in a book that had not been published . . . but I wish I had put a couple of quid on it.

Unfortunately, it seemed to say, this area cannot be ignored. I had a sinking feeling in the pit of my stomach which was soon reinforced by another visit from the unconscious.

I dreamt that I was witness to an IRA attack. I tell the police, and then get caught by the terrorists. I am tried and sentenced to be burned to death. I am taken up to a roof by an obviously gay guard who touches me up on the way. When we step out on the roof I knock him to the ground and kick him in the face. I see a prayerbook lying nearby, pick it up and ram it down his throat, holding it there with the heel of my hand until he chokes to death. Then I climb over the edge of the building and escape . . .

I was quite impressed with my tactics, until I heard David Kay's first response. "Why are you trying to kill what you perceive to be your homosexual side?" I didn't have an answer. When David spoke of the possible links between the homosexual side of the psyche and creativity, I thought he was saying I was gay, and pointed out all kinds of "proof" of heterosexuality. It took me a while to calm down.

In the meantime I had to take my confusion with me to Westminster Abbey for the first of two ceremonies. This one was to place my father's ashes into the ground. I sat in Poet's Corner trying to keep a dignified front, as I listened to the simple readings. The sympathetic looks from family and friends seemed full of hidden meaning—as if they knew all that was spinning inside my head. I held my three-year-old son on my knee and, at the end, walked with him and my mother to place flowers in the square opening, on top of the urn. As the flowers hit the bottom of the shallow hole, I turned to see him looking at me, a quizzical expression on his face, as if to say, "What's up?" I silently answered him, "I don't know—yet. But I will find out, because if I don't, you may have to do it for me—and that wouldn't be fair." Tears sprang to my eyes as I stood there, over my father's ashes, in between mother and son. I squeezed his hand and led him back to our seat. We would be returning here in a week's time to unveil the stone that would entomb my father forever in this holy place. Before then I would be helping to organize the men's conference with Robert Bly and Michael Meade, called, appropriately enough, "The Shadow and the Soul." Maybe that would shed a little dark on the situation.

Chapter Nine

The Shadow of Betrayal

Each of us contains both a Dr. Jekyll and a Mr. Hyde, a more pleasant persona for everyday wear, and a hiding, night-time self that remains hushed up most of the time. Negative emotions and behaviors—rage, jealousy, shame, lying, resentment, lust, greed, suicidal, and murderous tendencies—lie concealed just beneath the surface, masked by our more proper selves. Known together in psychology as the personal shadow, it remains untamed, unexplored territory to most of us.

(Connie Zweig and Jeremiah Abrams,
from the introduction to *Meeting the Shadow*)

I discovered the hard way that the Shadow (my own darker self) does not want to be known or seen. Like some hammy Dracula in a bad B movie, it sucks lifeblood in the dark, shies away from the light and shifts its shape. Every time I come to write about this particular weekend, it changes. What seemed clear the last time has become obfuscated, ridiculous; while completely new memories and "obvious" interpretations pop to the surface with alluring ease. To be honest to the experience a certain uneasy confusion must remain, even now.

MELTING THE STONE

Wendell Berry puts it like this:

TO KNOW THE DARK

To go in the dark with a light is to
  know the light.
To know the dark, go dark.
Go without sight, and find that the dark, too,
  blooms and sings,
and is traveled by dark feet and dark wings.
  (from Wendell Berry, *Farming: A Hand Bookayay*)

Part of the shadow's power comes from its unknowableness, and if that essential mystery is not respected it can deliberately mislead you, just for the hell of it. As I found out.

I arrived at our conference venue, Gaunt's House, in a state of nervous exhaustion. I was in the middle of directing four productions on the trot, and alternately trying to come to terms with my father and explore the allegations of homosexuality which had worked their way so deeply under my skin. Any concern I had that an organizing role would limit imaginative participation in the event was quickly put to rest thanks to the first part of a fairy tale entitled "The Princess and the Tree."

A young man, working as a pigherder, one day lookayayed up and saw a huge tree he had not noticed before. He started to climb it to see what the view would be like from the top. He climbed for a whole day, and then slept in the branches. He climbed for a second day and slept in a village he found there. He climbed for a third day and came to a great castle inhabited by a beautiful Princess. She invited him to stay the night, and said he was welcome to lookayay in all the treasure-filled rooms—all except one which had a closed door. To this room entry was forbidden. The next morning the young man explored the castle, until he came to the forbidden door. But then, almost without thinking about it, he found his hand was turning the handle and the door was opening . . .

Michael Meade abruptly stopped drumming—and asked us to close our eyes, imagine that door swinging open, and see what lay behind it—for us.

I closed my eyes, saw a large wooden door with iron hinges, which creaked open to reveal a hideous, huge, witch-like creature, with four arms swirling round her fat body and a blackened tongue protruding from her cracked mouth. Her face was hairy and she wore a twisted smile beneath her piercing eyes. There was another figure in the room behind her. A man in a glass case shaped like a coffin was hanging on a wall. He was still, his hands on his chest in prayer position with a small object between them. He was wearing a silver-white top with a red crusader's cross over the chest, and a strange cone-shaped hat, like a bishop's mitre, on his head.

It was clear and immediate, as if it had been waiting for me. I quickly sketched it on a notepad. It was disturbing and left me vulnerable and strangely excited. What did it mean? I lookayayed at my drawing and saw a powerful, devouring mother and a ghostly father. Robert Bly suggested our image was from behind a door that we were not supposed to open in our lives. It was trapped within us, and was currently blocking our growth. Oh shit.

Having recently faced up to examples of the weak masculine, the strong feminine, and homophobia in the outer world, I felt I was now meeting them again in my own Shadow. *A Dictionary of Symbols* lists homosexuality as:

> Symbolic of an inadequate conscious relationship with . . . a man's anima. This may have arisen, in the past, from an over-powering figure of the opposite sex . . . instilling fear of that sex, or an inadequate figure of the same sex—often the parent—giving insufficient support for the dominant physical characteristics to gain equivalent hold in the mind . . .

It seemed as though I was not yet out of the forest, and silently prayed there were no closets lurking nearby. Of course, in one sense the shadow itself is a closet, symbolized in the story by a "forbidden room." I had stepped into this room with homophobia; what my soul would emerge from it with, remained to be seen.

In the fairy tale, the young man finds a large black raven nailed to the wall behind the door. He obeys its request to feed it some water, whereupon it changes into a black magician and disappears. The next morning the young man wakes up back at the bottom of the tree, wondering where the Princess had gone.... He has seen feminine beauty, but has not yet earned the right to be with her. And what stood in his way was a black magician, who represented his own shadow.

Robert Bly described the shadow as "the long black bag that we drag behind us." He asked us to imagine that we came into this world with "a fully rounded 360 degree personality . . . with energy radiating from all parts of our body and psyche." At birth we were given a large bag to carry around. As we grow up we take unwanted slices of our 360 degree personality and put them in the bag. Our parents are usually first to decide which parts of us are "acceptable" and which are not—some manage to accept more than others. So we dutifully "bag" these parts to retain approval. Then we go to school, where teachers help us fill the bag some more. The teenage peer group later takes over from authority figures, and more slices go in the bag. By the time we leave school this bag is pretty full. "We spend the first twenty years of our lives filling the bag with stuff—and the rest of our lives trying to get it back out."

A large amount of vital energy is necessary to control the stuff in the bag. While this energy is used to keep the shadow hidden, it is unavailable to make informed individual decisions in daily life. As Rudolf Hoss, the Commandant of Auschwitz, wrote in his autobiography:

It was constantly impressed upon me in forceful terms that I must obey promptly the wishes and commands of my parents, teachers, and priests, and indeed of all grown-up people including servants, and that nothing must distract me from this duty. Whatever they said was always right. These basic principles by which I was brought up became second nature to me . . .

Ergo big bags cause big trouble.

The opening of this bag is a tricky business. It is not popular with friends, family, or society in general. Jung said, "Those parts of us that we do not love, regress." If we put slices into the bag at the age of five, and try to get them out at the age of thirty-five, they will be angry and neglected. It may be dangerous to do alone, precisely because the anger is undefined. As I had found out, it was easy to yell at people, more difficult to yell at the right people. In order to get to the jewels that lie at the bottom, you have to go through a lot of shit.

The men's stories this weekend seemed living proof of this. They were darker and deeper. When we brokayaye up into our small groups one man introduced himself, and spokayaye of feeling "invisible." As if to emphasize his point, I had already forgotten his name. I edged closer to him in my chair, anxious to show more interest in whatever else he might say. The acting was unnecessary.

After the war, I went to live with my grandparents in Dresden. My father had been killed on the Russian front and my mother lived in a different part of Germany. I was seven.

One day I was walking along the street with my grandmother, lookayaying into shop windows, when she suddenly said that I had dark circles under my eyes, and asked me if I was playing with myself. What did she mean? I had no idea. For the next two days she continued asking, and I always denied it. But I couldn't keep up my resistance. And so, believing that the persecution would then end, I confessed to doing that which I did not even know how to do.

But this was only the beginning. I was to be prevented from "abusing myself" at all costs. Every morning I was inspected for the "tell-tale" dark circles under my eyes, and many mornings they "proved" me guilty. My grandfather had now been pulled into the conspiracy, and would plot strategies with my grandmother. One night they filled some ski mitts with nails and pins and made me wear them in bed, so any movement of my fingers would cause sharp pain. This became a routine. The morning inspections, however, did not cease, and I was often still found guilty. I was a child with light, translucent skin. I was just a boy who had dark circles under his eyes. But they refused to believe me.

My grandfather would be told about my supposed nocturnal activity every evening on his return from work. I would be in the room, playing on the floor, usually under the table, and overheard these conversations, which would end with further strategies plotted; more pins, sharper nails, hands tied to the side of the bed, etcetera.

By this time I, too, was convinced that I must be doing this dreadful thing, without being aware of it. I continued living with my grandparents for another two years, always subject to the ski mitts. When I was reunited with my mother, the ski mitts were never mentioned again. They disappeared from my life as if they had never existed.

For years I carried this secret around inside me. I did not know how deeply I really felt about it, and what a profound effect it had had on my life . . .

When he finished we sat in stony, sympathetic silence. I wanted to jump up and embrace him, tell him that it was OKAYAY—but the story had been related with such dignity and control that even a manly slap on the back would have felt intrusive. Funnily enough Stephen, for that was his name, said later that he had wanted some support, but always felt unable to ask for physical comfort. After an experience like that, I'm not surprised.

Later on, back in the large group, men began to relate stories that increasingly revolved around fathers and abuse. One man told a complicated tale of serial abuse in his family, going back several generations. As he spokayaye, it seemed a weight was lifted off him. He had struggled with this unknown burden all his life; for the past year he had carried it alone, consciously, and now the very act of speaking the dark secret in this setting was lightening his load. His determination to end the cycle of abuse was absolute. A hundred men silently lauded his bravery. This one, at least, wished for some of the same spirit.

Another man, recently separated from his family, spokayaye of a terrible fear he had had that he would abuse his children when they came to visit him. He sought therapeutic help and was able to recall deep buried memories of the abuse he had suffered at the hands of his father. He pulled himself out of the heartfelt pain visible in his face to utter a single, damning statement: "I'm here to tell you that that kind of behavior *is fucking out of order . . .* !"—his finger jabbed powerfully forward as barely controlled rage echoed around us. He stood there, quaking. The room froze, as if in tribute to a moment he had claimed his own. Then his body seemed to soften, relax, as he finished quietly: "I just want to say that I still love my father . . ."

Here was a living example of Alice Miller's insistence on anger before forgiveness, feeling before healing. The whole atmosphere in the room filled with childhood secrets and betrayals, as more men spokayaye of things "forbidden." By the end of the evening I was quaking in my trainers, and deeply worried about what my memory might throw up in this setting. I quickly joined a couple of friends, and a bottle of Scotch, for a moonlit walk across nearby fields. Later veiled lookayays told me that I had imbibed more than my fair share. It wasn't my fault—I was thirsty. But whatever shadows were slouching towards consciousness were not going to be put off by a mere half pint of Knockando.

MELTING THE STONE

By the time I had carefully avoided the pre-breakfast yoga work-
out, I had almost persuaded myself that some horrendously abusive
paternal betrayal was waiting for me. No such luck.

A STORY

Sad is the man who is asked for a story
and can't come up with one.

His five-year-old son waits in his lap.
'Not the same story, Baba. A new one.'
The man rubs his chin, scratches his ear.

In a room full of bookayays in a world
of stories, he can recall
not one, and soon, he thinks, the boy
will give up on his father.

Already the man lives far ahead, he sees
the day this boy will go. 'Don't go!
Hear the alligator story! The angel story once more!
You love the spider story. You laugh at the spider.
Let me tell it!'

But the boy is packing his shirts,
He is lookayaying for his keys. 'Are you a god,'
the man screams, 'that I sit mute before you?
Am I a god that I should never disappoint?'

But the boy is here. 'Please, Baba, a story?'
It is an emotional rather than logical equation,
which posits that a boy's supplications
and a father's love add up to silence.

(Li-Young Lee, from *City in which I Love You*)

Memories stirred. I was back around endless silent dinner tables, late at night, alone with my father: I was waiting for tales, for stories, for wisdom—all in vain. He would sit with his head in his hands, bearing the burden of his life lightly in his palms; then lookayay up and smile, sweetly, helplessly, as if to say, "I know you want something from me, but I can't help you, sorry . . ." I would be doing the silent urging, "come on, Dad, please, tell me things, help me to understand the world, you, me, anything . . ." Now, in the light of this poem, I wondered what he had thought of those times. What was he feeling behind that chiseled face, kept so oddly young by wasting illness?

Then, suddenly, I knew. The inability to speak came from a deep-rooted belief in his inadequacy off the stage. In family life, performance was not appropriate. He could communicate to a thousand strangers with ease, but not to one son. I was on the verge of blaming again when another veil lifted. He had paid to educate me beyond his sixteen years of schooling, and then felt, yes, stupid, in my presence. He was afraid any comment from his emotive, intuitive self would be shot down by my arrogant intelligence, which was my best—only—defense against his greatness. He felt that I had already gone beyond him and would not seek to drag me back; I felt infinitely inferior and saw his silence as further proof of my worthlessness—"Surely if he thought I was worth it, he would speak . . ." And so we were both diminished by the other at the very times we could have been enlarged. The longing of these moments had, indeed, ended in silence. But I had contributed to the awkward tension and had often chosen to ignore the undercurrent of love, unspokayayen and unacknowledged, that flowed from him.

Many modern fathers may face a similar unfair burden of filial expectation: "Am I a god that I should never disappoint?" Unfortunately, there is a real sense in which they *are* a god—to the son. In ancient societies the established male line led from son to father, to other older men, to a king and then to a god. But trust in mentors, kings, and religion has been whittled away, leaving the father to carry the torch of masculinity by himself. In the absence of these other figures, the son expects the father to be the mentor, the king and the god. This leads to a certain amount of confusion, not to mention disappointment. Traditionally the father would never be expected to help choose the son's career. It was accepted that this was the job of the mentor. The father feeds you but does not "see who you are." The mentor points you in the right direction but has no responsibility for your well-being.

Without this kind of clarity, I had first assumed my father would teach me everything about the world and my place in it; when he inevitably failed, I found a mentor, the film director Tony Richardson, whom I assumed would be a substitute father. Not content to watch and learn, I wanted to be a pampered son. When Tony offered to produce a small film for me to direct, I childishly waited for him to do all the work, instead of allowing his encouragement to spur me into action.

Some fathers present asked if they could avoid disappointing their sons. "Should we tell them early on that we are not perfect?" Michael Meade disagreed: "It'll happen—just be ready for it. It's no good saying, 'I'm inadequate.' The son will turn round and reply, 'I know you're fucking inadequate—I just want to know if you have a heart' or something." Sons are waiting to hear how the father's heart was brokayayen, and about his mistakes, for this will make the father more human.

We went back to the story.

The young man tracked down the Princess, but found she was living with the black magician. He tries to escape with her but they are easily found by the magician and his magic horse. In order to find out how to acquire such a horse, the young man spends a night under the bed that the Princess shares with the black magician . . .

As we were asked to put ourselves in the young man's place, for many of us the bed quickly changed into the bed of the parents. A reminder of the early Oedipal battle where we yearn for mother's total love, and try to outwit this other dark, mysterious figure, father.

And then—while other men spokayaye of their helplessness at hearing parents' sexual activity—I saw it. The dark thing that had been waiting for me this weekend—my betrayal of the father. As a teenager, on some psychic level, I had won the battle for the mother and taken the father's place.

When my mother had lookayayed to me for some help in dealing with the family situation, although some part of me knew it was strange, another part had lapped up the attention and power it gave me. When my father was too frail to decide how to spend his time, my mother and I had decided for him. And I had enjoyed it. I had relished the victory and the fact that, in those moments, she was mine and I was preferred over him. She would ask my advice. We would consult together at one end of the dining table, while my father became the child, helplessly lookayaying on from the other. I remembered, with a shudder, the flashes of bitter resentment that would pass across his face as he struggled to even hear the plans we were making for him. And the sadistic pleasure I had felt in not repeating them louder so he could participate, or dare to refuse. I had reveled in the opportunity to punish him, for being away, for being ill, for taking mother away to work, whatever it was.

I started feeling queasy—and it wasn't just the hangover. It was as if I had opened the lid of a sewer to have a quick lookayay, but the pressure from underneath had forced it from my hand. Now the foul liquid was oozing around my feet. I was full of feelings of self-doubt. "Surely not. Not me. I'm just a nice boy. I don't feel these things. Hate my father? Uh-uh. You've got the wrong person. You must be looking for someone else . . ."

But the feelings wouldn't go away. Guilt mixed with hate in a poisonous cocktail, until, weary of the struggle and fearful of what further resistance would bring, I swallowed the awful truth. I had felt all these things, had done all these things. It was in me.

The beginnings of acceptance helped. The panic subsided—leaving gut-wrenching spasms of aftershock, but no danger of suffocation. I felt ungrounded, as if the proverbial carpet had been pulled from under my feet. My moral stance of "aggrieved victim" had been sent sprawling.

I felt the reverberations of this ripple through the rest of the day's conference. While the young man in the story was accomplishing tasks for a witch to gain a magic horse, my mind turned back to the image I had seen behind the forbidden door.

I had started by naively assuming, even hoping, that I would be lookayaying at my parents' shadows. Now I had to take responsibility for my own shadow. My initial impulse—to project the uncomfortable stuff out onto others—was a natural one, but had not been ultimately helpful. I could no longer identify the figures behind the door as mother and father. That was too easy—too safe. I realized they were part of me too. In the story the witch keeps the magic until the young man has earned it. Maybe the imprisoned male figure, half crusading knight, half priest, held some magic that I would have to earn.

That afternoon provided a vital clue and then simultaneously covered it with a thick smokayayescreen. Our small group, under Stephen's increasingly visible and welcome leadership, decided to do some physical work together, which culminated with the "falling leaf" trust exercise. I had a sudden Buffalo Gap flashback and bravely opted to go last.

When I was finally lifted off the ground, some impulse made me act out the knight-priest from behind that door. I stiffened my body and held my hands as if in prayer. I was floating in the air, weightless, when I remembered that there had been something in between those hands. I struggled to recall the image and see what it was, quietly hoping for something butch like a sword. The mist cleared, to reveal a bookayay. Fair enough, I thought, as I swayed in the air, supported by twelve hands. I felt light, almost peaceful—until I registered a fearful niggling at the back of my head; a data recovery system going into overdrive. I started my descent back to the ground, floating gently down, when some logical part of my mind decided the bookayay should be a prayer bookayay—which set the cat among the pigeons.

The earth became solid under my body. I opened my eyes to see six heads standing giant-like over me, silhouetted against cloud scudded sky. I was pulled to my feet by strong hands, but as the others headed into the dining room I lagged behind, needing time to think.

A series of wild associations were set off. The two reference points I had to prayer bookayays were the prayer bookayay I had used as a weapon to kill a gay guard in a recent homophobic dream; and the prayer bookayay I had placed on my father's coffin, which had been given to him by his father, an Anglican priest. To this strange concoction I added the Danny Kaye allegations and my homophobic reaction. And the forbidden door, hiding a witch imprisoning a passive man who was connected with religion and holding a bookayay. At that moment I came to my unprovable assumption, that I was facing some kind of repressed homosexuality in the Olivier male line.

I was quite excited by this hypothesis, for a while. I had solved the mystery, got to the bottom of my homophobia. It was nothing to do with me, it was all passed on down the family line.

It was not until much later that I saw the trap I had fallen into. I had come into this event with my own agenda, to find somebody to blame for my homophobia, and I had finally managed it. But I had not seen the shadow creep into my fantasy "solution," then slope off sniggering at my gullibility.

Having tried only hours before to pull back a bit of shadow projection I had thrown at my father, and accept my part in our distance, I had been only too willing to blame his father, my grand-father, for my current confusion. Marvelous. I could see how some people might come up with fantasy abuse stories in therapy, par-ticularly if the therapist and patient start to anticipate the possibility. It is as if our shadow says, "Be careful of what you are lookayaying for—you might just get it!"

I had got it. Luckily I had seen through it; though no other ideas sprang up to replace it. I would have to live with the mystery of those figures behind the forbidden door, not knowing what they wanted from me. I would have to pry my interpretive claws from them, let them breathe, even water them—wait and see what they held in store for me.

Two days later I arrived at Westminster Abbey, trying to draw comfort from Robert Bly's parting words, "It is more important to be in the right place than to solve problems. To be in an authentic dilemma is a tremendous piece of luck . . . !" I hoped so.

I tookayay my seat around the edge of Poets' Corner, and was grateful I had no official part to play at this ceremony. There were no performance nerves to interfere with my private experience. I wondered what my father would make of all this. His usual Gemini split, I supposed; caught between "quite right too" and "get me out of here quick, before everyone realizes the mistake!" But as we bowed our heads in prayer, a quickening in my solar plexus told me that I was not just here to enjoy myself; there was work to be done.

I silently summoned my father's spirit to be present to hear my thoughts—tried to banish doubt and embarrassment at the effort—shut my eyes, and began . . .

"Hello, Dad, there are some things I wanted to say to you, and this felt like a good opportunity. Maybe the last one.

"I've been going through a great deal since you died, but some-how I think you knew that. I got stuck. Trying to run away from you so fast I kept tripping up and tying myself in knots. Well, in the last few days I realized part of the reason I was running. Because I did not want to face my guilt. I have found plenty of cause to be angry with you, and though I never had the courage to express it to you while you were alive, I have discovered a way to release it even though you are no longer here.

"But now I've come to say sorry to you; for betraying you, for taking your place, unearned, in the household, and being so cruel with it, for rubbing in my position of power, for flashing the throne I usurped from you in front of your eyes, whenever I could. For resenting your weakness, your age, rather than appreciating your strength and courage in simply remaining alive, against all the odds. For competing with you, endlessly, for everything—and every time I won, thinking you the lesser for it. I needed to find a way to diminish you in my mind, to shrink you from the giant stature everyone told me you filled, to a man I could more easily hate—and therefore more humanly love.

"And I want to thank you. For all the ways you did father me that I did not see, or want to see at the time. For coming into my room every night you could when I was young to strokayaye my back and send me to sleep. I would want to stay awake just to enjoy your touch, your presence. But I knew you wanted me to go to sleep, and so I would pretend to be asleep so you could leave. Thank you for your patient trips to far off playing fields to watch me in school teams. I am sorry I did not acknowledge you then, or appreciate your effort. Thank you for encouraging me to go to college in America, and for traveling there with me to help make it possible. Thank you for visiting me there, even when you were really too ill to travel. Thank you for loving me the best way you could. I used to go around thinking it was not good enough, because it did not happen according to my wishes. But you did not disinherit me. You left me to find my own way. I thank you. I forgive you, and I ask forgiveness of you. I do not ask it easily or expect it quickly. But when it comes—if it comes—I will know, for I will have been twice blessed by you. In my life, and in my living. Farewell, Father . . ."

MELTING THE STONE

My eyes were wet. I opened them to see the velvet cloth slowly slipping away to reveal the stone slab that had entombed my father's earthly remains. I felt something dark and heavy leave my body, some guilty shade released from prison. I thought that my father had taken on some of the stone I had been burdened with for so long. It was right that his life and achievements should be immortalized in stone, wrong that a boy should be petrified before his life had really begun. I walked out of that ancient place a little taller, lighter—perhaps even free.

Chapter Ten

Re-membering and Re-turning

Honor had been paid. I felt I had willingly given respect which previously I had grudgingly withheld. I had made the treacherous journey into the father's house, and even done a little redecorating. But this was to prove only the first stage of an unending adventure in which, as they say, "It is better to journey in hope than to arrive."

I had come to see my father, finally, as a human being. Now I had to face the psychic legacy he had left me, or, more accurately, the curse a teenage boy imagined that legacy to be. After that I would find a hidden blessing to turn my head towards the future, to leave his house and find my own. These tasks were just as slow, gruesome, and frightening as those which went before. Indeed, many of the skirmishes were the same—old enemies revisited. It was as if I was on two spiraling loops simultaneously, going round to meet the same view but from a slightly different angle. And only getting a bit further up the top one if I descended further on the bottom one.

MELTING THE STONE

A few weeks after unveiling my father's stone at Westminster Abbey, I dreamt of him alive, old but not ill, for the first time since his actual death. He walked into a room at the country cottage and we were both pleased to see each other. After a bit I left him to have a meal, while I went outside with some friends. David Kay wrote about this dream that, "because the father is no longer a dead, destroyed object in your inner world, the ability to start a mourning process has been achieved, and, through that, the possibility of separation and existence in your own right as a man."

Which sounded pretty good. Until, a month later, I was reminded why I had spent most of my life avoiding these "mourning processes." They bloody hurt.

The day before I had to fly to Vienna for a production week, Shelley and I got a call at home to say that Jonathan Murro, the priest who had married us, had been found dead. He had apparently hanged himself. I was shocked, stock still—but spinning inside: "Priests don't commit suicide, they don't give up, not like that . . ." But I did not let myself feel too much. A little concern. A little sympathy. Nothing more. I had a show to do, for God's sake. My schedule had no room for death. Yet.

Three days later, sitting in a darkened auditorium in Vienna, I was handed a message to call Tony Richardson's house in Los Angeles. I had a brief flash of foreboding which I dismissed. Until I made the call and heard the tone in the voice that answered. Tony was in the hospital dying of Aids. He was not expected to last through the night. I mumbled into the mouthpiece as best I could, and hung up.

I sat motionless, staring at the plastic messenger of doom. My vision narrowed, as I tried to make it and its message disappear. But it remained obstinately present. My chest began to throb with unfamiliar urgency. My brain responded instantly, shooting adrenaline into the bloodstream to repel the unwanted intruder. The two locked in combat, the brain sensing habitual victory, yet surprised at the ferocity of the heart's struggle for freedom. Images of my

188

dying friend, mentor and substitute father alternately appeared and crumbled before me. Even as I swam in this sea of emotion, I could sense the brain fighting, resenting it still. I ignored it—determined to send telepathic love to a hospital room six thousand miles away.

Then an assistant came into the office—I was required on stage. I turned my back on the phone, wiped my eyes and walked towards the auditorium. The show must go on.

Not even "Dr. Theater" could cure this complaint. The next day I was told that Tony had, indeed, died. The sensation came back, heavier, harder to bear. I held the grief—not wanting to unload it but unaccustomed to it's sorrowful weight. Maybe in grieving for my great friend, I was finally grieving for my father.

I returned to England, but couldn't explain to Shelley what was going on. I began to feel lost, isolated, depressed. And embarrassed. Nervous about not being in control of my emotions, and ashamed that I did not seem to have the language to express them, even to an intimate partner. I had lost the man who married us, and my best man, Tony, in the space of a week. I began to fear for the health of the rest of the wedding party, until my unconscious came to the rescue.

I dreamt that Shelley and I were getting married again, in Tony's garden, but without him or Jonathan Murro present. There was no official ceremony, but our friends bore silent witness to our marriage. At the end I turned to Shelley and said, "I couldn't feel it fully before—I can now."

The pain and isolation of losing Tony however, also held out the promise of joy and greater union in my marriage. I was learning the hard way you can't just increase the capacity to love without simultaneously increasing the propensity for pain. Which was, of course, a good enough reason for the child to have limited both in the first place.

I was still crossing a minefield—but instead of walking with a blindfold on, I was now crawling through the mud with a metal detector. It started bleeping soon after my thirtieth birthday. I came down with bronchitis, which heralded the return of a teenage complaint, asthma. I was intrigued, not to say pissed off, and looked around for my deerstalker. The asthma had started when I was thirteen. I started scanning memory tapes for that year. Twice they ground to a terrified halt.

One concerned a visit to see Dad in hospital where he was suffering from dermatopolymyositis. Nobody had ever said that he might die, but I had sensed something more than usually wrong, and wanted to find out for myself. On a weekend home from boarding school I went to the hospital, found the right ward, crept along to his room and opened the door.

He was sitting up, struggling to get out of bed, and swearing loudly as he ripped tubes from his body. I stopped, but it was too late, he had sensed my presence. He turned to face the intruder, rage blazing out of piercing hard, gray eyes. I didn't wait to see if he recognized me. I turned and ran out of the door, trying to wipe the nightmare image of the mad, dying father from my mind, and shouted for a nurse. She came, running, and rushed past me into the room, leaving me staring through the moving rectangular window as the door swung back and forth, revealing then hiding the absurd struggle within. I wanted to stay, wanted to say something, do something, but I was hopelessly out of my depth. And I didn't want to face the devil in those eyes again. I slunk away, beaten, helpless and alone.

He wrote of this time:

> The disease . . . turned out to be rather scary . . . All that anyone knew, apparently, was to feed it with steroids in large doses; but such very large doses can have an alarming effect. I actually went out of my mind . . . It was an appalling feeling, as if there was something right through my face and head turning at a steady pace round and round . . . churning like a wheel. I was obviously in great distress . . .
>
> (*Confessions of an Actor*, p. 325-6)

So was his son. Until he activated an emotional ejector seat and flew above the confusion, heading back to school sealed in stony sanctuary.

But the second memory revealed that there was no respite to be gained there. It was my first term in the senior school; there were boys up to five years older in the same dorm. New and bigger giants to be befriended or otherwise appeased. And one slightly older, much tougher boy whose affection I was destined not to win. I was the youngest in my year, a late physical developer, cheeky and fat. Perfect bait. It didn't take him long to bite. After he had seen me changing a few times he decided to start calling his mates in late at night. Then he would instruct me to drop my pajama bottoms, so they could laugh at my hairless genitals, mostly hidden by puppy fat. He never had to use force. I was too scared to risk resistance.

Even as I sat at my desk remembering those scenes, the shame came rushing down the years to catch me again. My head dropped out of eye contact, pulled down by the weight of burning cheeks. And some invisible body shrunk into the mold created by the teenage coward, feeling again my balls retracting like a sumo wrestler in trouble. As time wore on this comic relief was demanded less and less, but I lived in fear. Never knowing if mercy was due to his boredom or my diversionary tactics; bags of food stolen from home.

At the last men's conference we had endured a conflict session about class. Some men accused others of being lucky middle-class bastards. One riposte had been that children can also be "expensively deprived"—by nannies and boarding schools. I began to see how the latter can act as a "negative initiation." The sadism often encountered in such places prevents rather than stimulates true education. A true initiation occurs when an older male takes the boy away from the father and supervises fearful ordeals. These would extend emotional range and lead to creative independence. Separation, ordeals, return. My experience at thirteen had had the opposite effect. My father was apparently dying, certainly unavailable. The older male had been a sadistic bully; the trials set up for his entertainment, not for my education. So the fear did not lead to greater emotional depth, but further repression. Far from hard-won independence, I had become stuck in impotent boyhood.

As a result I came to distrust my potential. I was ways looking for someone else to help me; my father, my mother, Tony Richardson and other older friends. I interrogated my journal:

Why settle for others' dreams?
Why fly on fortune's wind
Riding the coat-tails of other men,
While blind to the clothes I wear?

Stop flying away—
Drop down—
Now!

Plummet those depths,
Before they close
And leave you in endless shallows.

I was scared to go out into the world on my own. I would soon be given a chance. Having taken over full organization of Mytho-po-etic Men's Conferences in England, in conjunction with Chris and Jackie from our small men's group, we started to bear the brunt of media and other inquiries. One result of this was a request to run an introductory day of men's work at Flint House, an alternative center in Lewes, Sussex.

I was nervous and inspired by the idea, and began to lay plans. But after Jackie canceled a couple of meetings, I became suspicious; when he pulled out, I got angry. This led to our first heated conflict at the next men's group. After a few sharp exchanges, which shocked the others, we were asked what was going on. We took a deep breath, eyed each other warily across the space and plunged in. I think if we, as the two instigators of the group, had not been able to talk through this miscommunication, the group itself would have been undermined. Perhaps it was this sense of responsibility to something bigger than ourselves that forced us beyond our normal defensive stances. We tried to speak honestly about the fears and needs that had brought us to this pass. It emerged that Jackie felt I was bullying him into something he was not ready for. His early experiences with groups of men had left him not wanting to put himself in the firing line until he was damn sure he would survive. I had assumed—without really checking—that since we had shared all our past experiences of men's work, we would naturally stick together for future developments. And I really wanted him to be there—I had got used to him being a kind of security blanket. We ended up both able to understand the other's position. It was the first visible difference in approach to this work, but it seemed containable. For now.

In any event I went ahead with the introductory day. But without the physical comfort of this "older brother," I planned conservatively, effectively hiding behind received ideas of others, rather than formulating my own. Even though it had been a step outside the father's house, it was too reliant on newer mentors.

But the conflict with Jackie had an effect on the group. We had been meeting for nearly a year; finally the trust was beginning to deepen. Our argument simultaneously stripped any covert leadership mantles from our shoulders, and tacitly gave permission for others to be forthcoming about grievances.

It was time for another shift. We invited in two new members, including Stephen, the former "invisible man" from the last conference. We decided to close our meetings (i.e. no guests), and name the group. After the usual prevarication (and heeding the warning offered by an infamous Californian group named, "The Hard and Fast Men") we settled on "Wild Dance." Since we didn't dance a lot and were rarely wild, this was more for inspiration than a branding.

We had settled into two sub-groups—the "Let's have a plan of action" boys and the "Let's just meet and see what happens" brigade—and were trying to find a way to contain both, when a small booklet arrived from the States. Entitled *Tending the Fire: the ritual men's group,* it was written by Wayne Liebman and sported an introduction by Michael Meade:

> Are [those who seek a group] simply looking for support and a therapeutic process? Or do they want the opportunity to struggle into a ritual alliance with no guarantee that their therapeutic needs will be filled in the group?
> . . . the ritual group is sustained by the willingness to wander along the uncertain edges of its terrain . . . [it] protects and nurtures all its members, yet benefits by uncovering and then encouraging the extraordinary capacities in each . . . It is the unusual, the rare, the abnormal, the extreme in each man that will develop from the uncertainty of the pursuit.

This offered us hope. It combined the promise of activity with the need for uncertainty. We were soon able to decide that we were a ritual group, and looked around for suitable material. Within a few weeks, Nigel—our other recent arrival—led us in an active imagination exercise to meet an animal. We would then make a mask of the animal's face and take it from there. I was intrigued by the idea, not least because it had nothing to do with anyone else. This would be ours.

I was determined to find a good-looking animal with strong legs, so it was my own fault I ended up with a snake. But over the next few weeks as we sculpted in Plasticine, applied the papier mâché, painted and glazed our masks, I came to appreciate its appearance.

When we actually came to put the masks on, I experienced a shocking joy. First to see these other men adorned with a creature from their imagination. As though we had claimed our right to be imaginative, creative beings, without shame or apology. Second to slip into the imagined character of the animal itself. To indulge in a bit of acting that would never be seen by any public but was just enjoyed for its own sake. For our sakes. And to learn from it. It was a seed of inspiration that would grow into the future.

As I slid around the room—occasionally self-conscious, but more often committed to the act—I was pulled into an unusual slowness. The slow motion sucked me towards quiet contemplation. This snake's patient strength and lowly slithering ways were the opposite of my habitual impatience, rising above and running away. Which was, of course, why it had appeared. I wanted to know more, but tried to learn its lesson, be patient and wait till next time.

So two weeks later, after our usual drumming and check-in, we donned the masks once more and headed off for another imaginative journey. This time to become the animal, and observe our human form coming to visit it. Then to see into the human's shadow, come back to the room and write about it:

MY HUMAN'S SHADOW

Self-conscious,
Self-important,
An aura of grandiose intensity
Protecting a thousand wounds—
A pierced shell
Like a gold digger's sifter
Drips out the confidence
He tries to retain.

A stone child lies within,
Untouched by passing years,
Immobile, yet screaming in silence.
Only tears can melt the rock,
Tears of grief,
Fountains of Life,
Can release the live boy
From the petrified shell.

Well, that was depressing. I hadn't consciously thought about what I was writing—simply described what the snake had seen. His vision was uncomfortably honest. I had wanted more information, but now I'd got it and didn't know what to do with it.

As the disturbing images began to pile up, I got the message: don't stop. I may have started to understand the situation, but— the snake insisted—that was not "solving" it. I was still looking for a miraculous cure for the stone child. Eventually I would have to learn simply to care for him. In a way that others had seemed unable to do consistently, earlier on.

These thoughts were fueled by the arrival of a long awaited letter from Irene, my first nanny, who had returned to Germany to get married when I was five. As I read through her enthusiastic description of my (apparently blissful) early childhood the question sprung into mind, "so what went wrong?" Momentarily caught off guard, an answer echoed back from the depths. "She left." I felt a low chord reverberate in the solar plexus. It had been so simple, it might just be true. In the face of a working father and a busy mother I may well have transferred affection to the nanny, with whom I spent the most time. When she left I lost my "substitute mother." Soon after I was sent to a strict school to deal with a growing discipline problem. It was a missing piece to the psychic jigsaw puzzle. An essential lesson in the small boy's education not to love too much; for anyone he really loved would go away. It was also a through line to the man's difficulty in consistently loving others.

Anxious not to be left alone with this, I quickly developed a cranky theory: the Oedipus Complex for Hooray Henry's. Subtitled, "Oedipus-schmoedipus, what does it matter? As long as a boy loves his Nanny." The traditional Oedipal impulse is to fall in love with the mother and hate the intruding father, who seems to have a prior hold over her. But if the first step is confused by a nanny who seems to replace the mother as primary caretaker/nurturer, then the other steps will be confused too. The mother, who is in charge of the nanny, giving orders etc., may replace the father figure. For she seems to have a prior hold over the nanny and be acting as the intruder in the nanny/son relationship. Meanwhile the often absent father is a step further removed from the son; being heard of but not seen. All of which might just leave the son wanting to fuck the nanny and kill the mother. Oops.

It would also overbalance the gender input towards the feminine. As I worked with these ideas, I felt the forbidden door from the shadow weekend swing open again. I was looking at an overbalanced feminine in the shape of the witch: her four arms seemed proof that she had the power of two women. She stood in between me and the masculine potential of the warrior priest. He who not only has beliefs but can stand up for them. What could I do to get by her?

I had been approached to see if I was interested in writing a book about the men's movement in England. Little did I realize it would be this task that held the clue. I was being held back by an overpowering image of the feminine which had been subconsciously created early on. This was standing in the way of creative masculine independence. While I was struggling with this dilemma I had another dream.

I was on a film set as an actor being directed by a gay friend, to act in a love scene with another man. I listened to the director, and then turned to embrace the other actor. It is a love scene rather than a sex scene, and I am able to relax and enjoy it.

I awoke feeling genuinely good about the dream; not guilty, worried, or threatened. It seemed that I had finally managed to get beyond my homophobia and accept that I, along with everyone else, had a homosexual side. And the only real danger was to go on pretending I hadn't. For then it would remain in the shadow bag and continue to cause trouble. The fact that homosexuality is connected to creativity was evidenced by being on a film set. And the acting was a way to access this side without becoming it or being "burnt" by it; which was, of course, the fear motivating the "gay murder" in my previous dream. Marie-Louise von Franz recommends dealing with the symbol of male homosexuality by "letting the Anima work as Muse on appropriate tasks involving feeling and imagination." And this, albeit unconsciously, was what I had been doing. Would my ventures into imaginative, creative realms stretch to writing a book? I had to take this question into the next men's event.

James Hillman and Michael Meade were at the helm—Robert Bly having claimed a year off. Both seemed to be on a new tack, luckily so was I. Hillman was launching a deliberately provocative book entitled *We've Had a Hundred years of Psychotherapy And the World's Getting Worse.* He accused traditional psychotherapeutic methods of sucking the energy out of the world, keeping people and their ideas trapped in the consulting room, rather than feeding the community around them. In danger of becoming prisoners of the past:

> If you are looking backwards, you are not looking around. The more you attribute what *is*, to what *was*—the more you are stuck in what *was*. We need to separate the past from causality. By taking the past literally, we believe that what happened earlier is most determinant. And therefore childhood becomes the most important part of life—which is absurd!

If we think that events in the past can determine our emotions and actions in the present, we actually give them the power to do just that. But if we could re-imagine our past as part of the given, instead of the main cause of the present, we would reduce the past's hold over us.

> Let's say that what matters is that you have an acorn in you, you are a certain person, and that person begins to appear early in your life, but it's there all the way through your life. Winston Churchill, for example, when he was a schoolboy, had a lot of trouble with language and didn't speak well. He was put in what we would call the remedial reading class. He had prob-

lems about reading, speaking, and spelling. Of course he did!
This little boy was a Nobel Prize winner in literature and had to
save the Western world through his speech. Of course he had a
speech defect, of course he couldn't speak easily when he was
eleven or fourteen—it was too much to carry . . .

Suppose you take it the other way and read a person's life backwards. Suppose we look at the kids who are odd or stuttering
or afraid, and instead of seeing these as developmental problems we see them as having some great thing inside them, some
destiny that they're not yet able to handle. It's bigger than they
are and their psyche knows that . . .

(*We've Had a Hundred Years of Psychotherapy*, p. 18)

As I tried to take this in, despite a veneer of resistance, there was a
huge wave of relief inside. A "let's hear it for the nerds" type of
thing. A validation that my times of oddity and fear may not simply have been the weakness I had assumed, but may actually have
had a purpose, for me.

Being in ritual space, my imagination and memory were nearer
the surface, and nearer each other than usual. I sent down a messenger with questions about weakness. He came back with a repeat
memory link of Dad in hospital and the dorm scenes of shame, but
with an addendum. What they led me to believe. A piece of the
teenage boy's "logic" came floating towards me: "My father is dying. I have to help him. He is a great man. I am nothing. I don't
need my creative, potent energy—people will only laugh at it in
me. Maybe I can give it to him—maybe then he will live . . ."

That way of course, not only was I doing something useful, but
I also could give up responsibility for moving out into the world
myself. Like the ape in my dream which had been blown up by my
parents, I envisioned myself as a sacrifice to a greater cause. A pawn
who could and would die to preserve the King. I later found an-
thropological support for this crazy logic, in a chapter of *The Golden
Bough* called "The Sacrifice of the Son":

> When the king first succeeded in getting the life of another ac-
> cepted as a sacrifice instead of his own, he would have to show
> that the death of the other would serve the purpose quite as
> well as his own would have done . . . No one could so well
> represent the king in his divine character as his son. . . . No one,
> therefore, could so appropriately die for the king . . . as the king's
> son . . .
>
> (J. G. Frazer, *The Golden Bough*, p. 289)

So I had followed a negative initiation through to its logical extreme. A positive initiation circumcises the male symbol of creativity,
and turns the penis into a phallus, full of future potency. In a negative initiation the knife slips, and the circumcision becomes
castration and impotence. I had imagined my own Faustian deal,
in which I gave up my potency, my tools of creative life, to increase
my father's life. And my father's unexpected survival was "proof"
that it was working. Any attempt to reclaim what had been given
up would surely kill him. If I became strong, I would lose father—
because our connection had occurred at the moment of mutual
weakness.

The day he died I had felt something intangible change. Now I
had a glimpse of what it was. My excuse not to grow up had died
with him. The potency I had imagined giving away was no longer
needed, and was available to be remembered. When I could figure
out what to do with it.

The next day Michael Meade weighed in with a talk on "Turning the head." He asked us to imagine two loops that meet in the
center, like an infinity sign. The loop on the left would be the Past
loop, connected to birth, childhood, the personal and family. The
loop on the right would be the Future loop, connected to adulthood, elderhood, the community and death.

Traditionally, initiation would occur when the elders of a tribe
thought a boy (or girl) was ready to turn their head from childhood to adulthood, from preoccupation with personal concerns to

responsibility for communal concerns. The initiation provided the clue to one's destiny —what Malidoma Somé called "finding the project of the rest of your life"—which was sealed with a wound. A literal cut or injury inflicted in the ritual space would mark the separation from the past, and remind the initiate of the task for the future.

But many modern men experience a wound much earlier on. Childhood traumas inflict a separation (or creation of a "false self"— which amounts to the same thing) before the child is ready to turn their head to the future. The pain of the separation and the apparent lack of meaning in it will leave the modern man either trying to permanently forget it, or trying to permanently repair it. Having done the former for twenty-seven years and the latter for four, I had intimate knowledge of both paths.

But what we take to be meaningless wounds—the cruel blows of fate—may in fact be defining moments for the future—the seeds of destiny. If we think of our wounds as the modern equivalent of the initiatory wound, we can find a message in the past to help us turn to the future. There is gold in the wound, and life is trying to come out of the wounded place. The "forgetful" man will not receive the message because he denies there is a wound—and therefore does not look back. While the "repairing" man does not accept the message because he assumes the wound was a mistake which must be rectified—and therefore does not look forward. Instead, we should redefine the wound, so it would no longer be the problem which stops us reaching our potential, but the only information we will ever get about that potential.

The attempt to cure the wound, which some types of therapy promote, would, from this point of view, be counterproductive. For if you could heal the past you would also wipe out the message. One of the things I had learned from meeting with groups of men is that being wounded is an experience we all share. The idea that it would be possible to have an unwounded childhood—and we were just unlucky—is in itself a childish fantasy, and patently untrue. It might actually foster an isolation, "I would be normal if I had not received this wound, but now I'm different and alone." The value of sharing tales of wounding, as we had done in these conferences and smaller groups, was in the community it created, "We're all in this together." The community in turn could then support and deepen the individual experience.

On the last morning I went for a walk by a nearby lake, struggling to put together the various ideas and images I had had so far. I was gripped by the unexpected arrival of a long buried memory.

I must have been about eight. I was working with my father, clearing boxes from cupboards at the top of our old house in Brighton. I asked him about acting. Did he think I should do it? He stopped what he was doing, paused for a moment, looking at me thoughtfully, and then said that the friend whose talent he most admired was Terence Rattigan: "because he can write. We actors only interpret words written by others—but to come up with the words themselves, to be a writer, that's true creativity. . . ."

At the time, of course, I was bitterly disappointed. I wanted to be told to be an actor and given inside info on how to do it. But, now, as the memory sunk in, I felt something shift within my chest, as if an invisible hand had struck me in the middle of my back. Suddenly I found myself full of gratitude. I sat on the wet grass and cried. He hadn't wanted me to give up my life or creativity for him. That was my invention. I no longer had to try and walk in his footsteps, or spend my life avoiding them.

I looked out at the lake and saw his face smiling at me down the years. The image began to fade, retreating to its rightful place. But normal vision was not restored. Instead I was faced once again with the forbidden door. Except I now felt bidden to open it. When I did there was no witch standing there, the warrior priest was standing at the back waiting for me. In his hands he held out a book towards me. In that moment I knew that my father had blessed this first step into independent creative life. I would write the book that I had been asked to write. However it turned out, it would lead into the future, and would seal off the past. Or rather turn the past into a story that could be told, instead of a bloody wound that could not be left. It would be, in itself, a turning of the head.

Chapter Eleven

Melting the Stone

As I embarked on this project I discovered in a very real way that there is no end to the search I had started. Those spiral loops keep on keeping on. But I was able to let go of the intensity with which I started, and step away from the childish need to be supported and applauded for everything I do. As Rumi wrote, "Start a huge foolish project, like Noah. It makes absolutely no difference what people think of you."

I had found a relationship with my father when I could help him, be of use to him; I had made my career out of helping and supporting other creative people. Now I had to create by myself. The long journey from feeling lonely to being alone had begun. It was not easy.

My resilience was tested on our first Wild Dance group expedition. And found wanting. We had agreed to meet for a walking weekend on Dartmoor. I had looked forward to it as a group experience. I ended up feeling paranoid, lonely, and unwanted. As we moved out across the desolate landscape, the jolly group split into straggling twos and threes. It became suddenly, stupidly, important whom I walked with. And if they singled me out for the next leg of the journey, or ended up with me by default. My psyche was back at boarding school, on long charity walks, trying to catch up with the people I wanted to be my friends, and trying to escape those who wanted to be friends with me. Again I was the one who tagged along unasked. Reliving the terror of going to school dinners too early. Of carrying my tray into a nearly empty friendless dining hall and being the first to sit at a table. Then pretending not to watch or care as friends and acquaintances came in and chose other empty tables rather than mine.

Now, aged thirty-something, I was still playing the same game, running an old school movie on the faces of the men I walked with. Feeling those who walked with me were simply suffering my company—would really much rather be with someone else. Grouchoesque—I would not want to be with anyone who would want to be with someone like me. Looking for people who would run away and running away from those willing to stay. I couldn't get rid of it, the depressing sensation was like a black hole, sucking any positive feelings out of the group experience, leaving me empty, hollow, still looking for something or someone to fill the gap.

When we returned to London I quickly set about planning our next venture a few months hence, determined not to repeat my particular role in the last one. This was to be on home ground, the group staying at my family's country cottage to facilitate a walk to a nearby ancient site, Chanctonbury Ring. I wanted ritual activities to be planned, to defend against loneliness. The group ended up in our old argument, unable and unwilling to agree on a schedule. And I was left without the structure I sought.

When the appointed time came some men arrived late, and kept up their casual chat. I resented it, feeling childishly that it "wasn't fair"; but knew complaining would have no effect except to further distract from ritual possibilities. We moved off and ascended the hill around the old pagan site. Everyone else seemed to be in a good mood, happy to mix frivolity with the golden sunset. I kept silently urging a swing to seriousness, wanting them to want what I wanted. Until finally I was forced to go off by myself to think and write alone.

What I realized, of course, was the value of being alone. And the danger of trying to mold others into a shape that may be right for me, but was not natural to them. As a ritual group we could support the eccentricities of the others, even value their extremes, but to try and make them bend to my will was another sign of immaturity. The grandstanding hero's need to be proved right. If I was a worthwhile person, a man of value, then I should not have to seek others' approval for my own interests. And I could learn things by myself.

I saw how my focus in the work we were involved in had shifted; from the conferences, to my analysis, and now to the small men's group. From inspiration, to understanding, and into experience. Now I had the chance to pull it back, into myself. Not to be selfish, but to stop being dependent. To give from a position of inner strength, not to make up for imagined weakness. To turn the black hole into a sun.

We returned from that ancient ring of trees and met in a circle in the moonlit garden, under a canopy of stars. I started getting a heavy burning sensation in my stomach. Something was brewing. It was not until I began to speak that it hit me. We were sitting on a patch of grass in a field, at one end of which stood the statue of the stone boy I had given my parents those years ago, and at the other end was the place I had dreamed an ape was found, killed and buried.

I had naively hoped that this group of men would help me magically rush over to the ape and revive it, instantly returning to me all that had been lost. But in truth where we were sitting right now was the right place to be, a little way away from the stone child, but not yet arrived at the wild ape, with his promise of creative spontaneity. The journey towards it was a personal one, may even take a lifetime to achieve. The rushing was the wish of the boy, who still believed he could magically become a man, if only. . . . But to live with the grief of this loss, and to take the painful task a step at a time, was a man's work. And the work itself was the making of the man.

This perception was deepened by the experience of the next conference, "Men: The Distance Between Us—The Distance Within Us," set up with Robert Bly and James Hillman. Recent biochemical research has shown that all fetuses are created feminine, until testosterone rushes in to create changes in those destined to become boys. Between this point (six weeks) and birth some 240 physical changes occur in the boy. Our first experience of being male is a chemical rush which manipulates us according to its own rules. As a result boys develop more slowly than girls, and some of the changes go on after birth. The next solely male experience was likened to exile, feeling thrown out of "the garden of Eden" when we realize we are not like mother. We have to disidentify with the mother's gender, and try to identify with the big brute reading a newspaper in the other gender corner. If we succeed in this, our second male experience is creating distance, and moving away from intimacy. If we fail to identify with father we may identify with another man, another woman, an object, or an ideal. However it works out, there is a tendency to treat people like things, and things like people. The inherent and automatic distrust of intimacy that so many men share, may stem from the pain felt on leaving the "paradise" of oneness with mother.

The first move is away from unity with something we love, and this wound may drive us all our lives. Many of us go to the opposite extreme, abstraction, and live with ideas and machines, anything that will not cause the same pain again. The desire for power and conquest may be driven by fear; of the loss we once felt and the vulnerable position we want never to be in again; perhaps even the wish for revenge, the bully's tactic of getting others to suffer the way he once did.

The feeling of this distance spread itself over the hundred men present. The fairy tale of "The Laddely Worm" provided the landscape through which we entered it:

> A Queen who wants a child ignores advice from an old woman and eats both a white and a red flower. Just before her golden-haired son is born, a little snake is delivered, but is thrown out of the window by a midwife. Years later when the golden boy travels towards his wedding, a huge snake appears in the road, and blocks his path. The snake declares he is the older brother, and he must be married first.

We were asked to think if we had such a dark brother. And to ponder the question, "Is there a being inside of me that does not wish me well." Men began to speak of the distance in their lives, of wanting to be with their kids but when the telephone rang leaving them all too easily, almost gratefully. Of arriving home late from work, falling into a loving hug with a patient partner, then spotting a pile of unimportant, unopened letters on a nearby table. And retreating from the threatened intimacy to the security of abstract busy-ness. All who spoke did not know what made them do this. It gave them pain, it caused pain to those they loved. It just felt like an unbreachable . . . distance.

The only comfort available was to know suddenly that this was a shared sensation. I was not the only man in the world to feel this way. I was not the only dad to leave my kids on the beach to go and read. I was not the only husband meanly to deny my wife an affordable treat. This did not excuse my actions, or justify them, but it somehow made sense of the helplessness I felt in their grip. It was extraordinary; I had always thought of myself simply as an unloving person, perhaps incapable of real love. Here I was no longer ashamed. No longer beaten by apparent lack. And it was not as simple as a failing. It was a difference; an essential reminder as we continue the gender debate that men are different from women. It will not help the situation to try and become something that we are not. We can learn from each others' strengths and weaknesses, not run from them, and not insist upon them. For distance can also be a strength, the ability to do necessary duty, to complete a dangerous task against the odds, to work through tiredness towards an essential goal. The trick is to find the balance.

My "dark brother" turned out to be a black baby, which swam into my mind and would not leave. When it revealed its source, I found, as in the story, that we shared the same mother. It was my source as well. When my mother became pregnant with me she was acting in *A Taste of Honey* on Broadway. Her character is pregnant, carrying the unwanted child of her black lover. For the first month of her real pregnancy my mother was using her creative imagination every night to believe that she was carrying a black baby that she did not want. And saying eight times a week with some intensity, "I hate motherhood . . . I'll bash its brains out. I'll kill it. I don't want his baby. I don't want to be a mother . . ." (*A Taste of Honey* by Shelagh Delaney, Act II Scene 2). I know that my parents had wanted me, but somehow I had always felt strangely unwanted and ashamed. Now I felt I had finally grasped a root of that feeling. My dark brother had started life as the imaginative creation of a brilliant actress, which a forming fetus may just have confused with himself.

Every subsequent rejection, however small in itself, had this dark brother to latch onto. Each shaming memory had fed this dark brother, who had grown to monstrous size. Becoming the voice in my head that told me I was unwanted, a nuisance, good for nothing. Making friendship dependent, and confidence impossible to maintain.

There were two unexpected gifts in his inheritance. First was the chance to release my mother from blame. This was not her fault, not part of a conspiracy to make me feel bad. She had simply been doing her job. Second was the fact of its creative origins. If the dark brother was a child of imagination, then it could have its head turned—could be initiated—by further imaginative work.

When this chance came, it was only appropriate that it should come through acting. On the last morning, at breakfast, Robert Bly asked me to assist him by acting the part of the Laddely Worm in the last part of the story. Initially, I refused, "Er . . . no thanks, I don't really act—I'm sure you can find someone better." But as I worried my cornflakes, I saw an opportunity. I knew the story, knew that this dark neglected brother would meet a bride who would demand he peel off seven layers of skin, to reveal the man underneath. If I could enter this imaginative play it may be a way to overcome some inner distance. I told Robert I had changed my mind. I spent the next hour or so trying to make use of the performance nerves shimmering through my body. And focus their attention on this dark brother.

When I stood up on the platform with Robert I was as ready as I would ever be; almost, but not quite, unselfconscious. I pulled my imagination around me like a protective cloak, blocking the hundred pairs of eyes out there, summoning the dark brother to leave his cave, infect me, invest me, become one with me. As the removal of the first skin was called for, my body tensed in expectancy. The first scream came from somewhere deep in the pit of my stomach, a sound I didn't recognize as mine. I urged it deeper still, to search out the primal sense of shame and scream it out. On and on it went, time dissolving in its wake. And when it was finished, exhausted, the second skin was demanded. And given; then the third, the fourth, and so on. By the end I was in tears, imaginatively inspired but truly felt. I was raw, bleeding, torn. Layers upon layers of angry defense stripped away, torn off, dropped down. And inside a vulnerable heart, sensing a release, beat with hope. When I stood up and looked once more around the room, I could see more clearly, feel more completely, as if perception had been cleansed, a new perspective given. It was the best, perhaps the only, true performance of my life. To do it, I had overcome an ancient fear that I could not act, that I was not good enough to act. I could, I was—when I needed to.

MELTING THE STONE

I knew that I could not actually change the past, but I could change the way that the past affects the present. And free myself from the imaginative conceptions that had so enchanted me and held me prisoner. And it had happened through a creative form of expression I had distrusted my whole life.

When I left the conference I began to plan workshops as theatrical events. The origin of the word theater is "to see," but I had been blind to its meaning, until now. By imagining myself a character, I had paid attention to something inside that had stood in my way. This dark brother was now offering me the gift of his creation, acting. This form could not only be used in ritual, it was ritual. The first actors were shamans channeling energies to the community they served. The first plays were symbolic reenactments of encounters with these forces. And this form of expression was part of my inheritance, not something in the past to run away from but part of a future to be worked towards.

The reverberations of this imaginative shift did not stop there, but moved through the maternal arena and into my marriage. I had puzzled over the fact that I had come to terms with father, but left my mother exiled, pushed away, perhaps out of fear of further smothering. Could I forgive my father for being absent, ill, and weak, but not forgive my mother for working, being strong and well? Or, worse, had resolution with father occurred *only* because he was dead, couldn't answer back, cause more trouble? Would resolution with mother only occur at her graveside? I hoped not.

It was a death that brought us back into relationship. Not hers but her mother's. When my grandmother died, I saw my mother cry, in private, in life—not in a play—for the first time I could remember. And as we all reluctantly moved one step further up the family ladder, something changed. I saw my mother suddenly not as a dominating woman trying to help/control me, but as an older woman who could use my help. And, also for the first time I could remember, I wanted to give it. Seeing her vulnerable, witnessing her ability to love and to grieve, which I had so often doubted, allowed something in me to open up.

My wife and children were away, but the rest of my family were back at the country cottage, facing another death. There was no press to deal with, no public face to mask private pain. This freedom allowed grief a depth, a richness I had not experienced before. A holding of the pain without seeking to offload it, get rid of it, or bury it. I helped Joan select the pieces to be read at the funeral, and agreed to read one. The service took place in Worthing Crematorium, five years and one month since we had been there for my father. I was a little older, maybe wiser. I sat beside my mother, held her hand, read the poem, cried as I did so and felt release. For my grandmother who had left before pain destroyed her natural dignity. For my mother who could grieve freely, without the distraction of fame. And for myself.

After the funeral, when I joined my wife and children in Spain, I was with them fully, completely. Pledging love to my wife with a freedom I had never known before. Not concerned with the past, or worried about the future; just there, in the present, in life; participating, not observing. When the distance came, when the intimacy became a threat, for the first time I was able to talk about it, and more often than not, move through it and re-engage.

There was an effortless flow between us, every gesture from one was reciprocated by the other. For five years we had come to this place. Every evening I could I would go for a swim in the cooling sea and watch the sun disappear into the water. They were near perfect moments, only incomplete because my beloved partner had not shared them with me. Until now.

THE GODDESS AT SUNSET

She watched bemused
As I waded out to sea,
Towards the glowing orb
Of the downward plunging sun.

MELTING THE STONE

I moved vigorously
To stir warm blood
And soothe icy veins.

Yet when I turned shorewards
And saw her approach,
I froze in love.

I couldn't believe it at first.
She was coming in to me,
The way I would come into her,

Giving of herself,
Overwhelming habitual instinct
That said cold was cold and that was that.

I glanced briefly at descending gold,
Then looked again
At the sunset in her eyes.

The magical apricot light
Played with her breasts
And illumined her smile—

Her face was iridescent,
Her body ethereal,
As my love left my heart
And enveloped her across the water.

The waves of feeling, at times of almost uncontainable joy, felt like a gift from my grandmother, from the maternal line. It was painful only in the knowledge that it could not last, go on for ever. Some distance, some work would interfere, and eventually some other death, at some other time, would seek to separate us. But the fear of those times must never again be allowed to get in the way of the present. Must not block the love that we have now. As someone once said, "It is important that when Death finds you, it finds you alive."

I had been granted the opportunity to feel once more, to melt the stone that had entombed my heart for so long, and step out into the world a still foolish but more passionate man.

Epilogue

A night full of talking that hurts,
my worst held back secrets: Everything
has to do with loving and not loving.
This night will pass.
Then we have work to do.

(Rumi, translated by John Moyne and Coleman Barks)

One of the reasons that I have been able to continue this work is that there are no dogma, no set of beliefs, and no gurus who must be obeyed. Although the conferences have supplied inspiration and information, and my analysis helped me understand the implications of my particular story, it is the small men's group where I continue to push boundaries and figure out how I relate as a man to the world I live in. And what's more it's free.

Various methods for working in groups and with ritual have inevitably evolved over the last fifteen years, many of which have been mentioned in this book. But every man can pick and choose which are suitable for him and/or his group and invent the rest. Which to my mind leads to a kind of healthy chaos, difficult to define and, more importantly, impossible to be led as a movement. To sit in a circle of men and listen to others, as well as practice talking honestly oneself, is a great gift. Especially if there is no pressure to be anything other than what you are, at that moment. No one to impress and no need to bullshit. The advice it took me a year to put into practice was the following:

"Get a group of between six and twelve men to agree to meet six times; include an older man—even if you have to drag him off the street; do some drumming, read some poems and fairy tales, talk—and see what happens. After six meetings anyone can leave, and the group can continue, expand, or finish. . . ."

Having focused almost exclusively on the benefits of such a group, it is only fair to point out the dangers. Trust is a slow business, you can't earn it or expect it immediately. And while it is important to respect the form of the meeting and the men taking part, this should not come before personal or psychic safety.

After a confusing newspaper article lumped together several disparate groups working with men, Wild Dance started getting phone calls from men deeply hurt by divorce and losing their children. And from others, angrier, who seemed to simply hate women, and were looking for a forum to express their hate. By the end of six meetings it should be possible to distinguish the "hurt" from the "hate." Hurt can move into grief which can lead to fuller future relationship; hate will be destructive to the group. Oh yes, and one deeply sensible men's outdoor adventure group in the States welcomed new members by shooting apples off their heads with a crossbow—until one~poor bastard got hit in the eye.

But, as Dr. Anthony Clare recently said, "You only get something abused if at its heart it is doing some good." This is as true of men's work as it is of psychology. An American colleague reported an alarming trend for underemployed therapists to set themselves up as men's workshop leaders, convince the men present they have problems and then offer to solve them privately at $50 an hour. As these ideas spread, quacks will jump on bandwagons and flog all manner of male panaceas.

In England I expect we will be less naive and more reticent. Which is, of course, both an advantage and a drawback. We are wary of the excesses of stereotypical American "Go-for-it-ism," and armed with natural cynicism. On the other hand we need not be put off by the lofty arrogance of those who reject new approaches on principle. A certain part of the English mentality will inevitably regard anything remotely connected with self-development and emotional release as criminal, up there with unfair play, murder, and success. No one I know is trying to use this work to start a new religion, attack women, restore the patriarchy, or make men more savage.

The work, for me, is in three parts: past, present, and future. Or—possibly—history, culture, and destiny. Until we know where we have been, and where we are now, we will not know where we can go. For a period of time this work is selfish. About *me* and *my* feelings. Necessary because they have been hidden in the shadow and disowned, and must be reclaimed. But if it stays there too long it becomes self-obsessed, the adult version of the high-chair tyrannical baby who believes he is the center of the universe. As Robert Moore says, "You may be a beautiful planet; but you are not the sun!" The work starts moving out into the family and then the community. The point of departure will often be inspired by the wound found in the past.

There is an Inuit myth of the making of a shaman in which the potential healer is dismembered and his body parts dropped into the underworld, where various demons come and gnaw on his bones. Then the bones are brought back, put together and the subject revivified. He is now a shaman but can only heal those people who are afflicted by the demons who chose to gnaw on his bones.

There is gold in the wound. Possibly then, the more wounds we suffer, the more gold we may find. The more demons that have eaten away at us, the greater our capacity to help others. Which gives a little hope. Maybe.

I was gnawed on by the demons of fame, and I see a great deal of danger around in a culture where fame is so sought after. Especially by the young for whom it can become an aim without any further purpose. Having been brought up in a household connected with fame, I know that, in and of itself, fame solves nothing. It is often a quest for attention or admiration, a need to be recognized and to feel a part of something. Unless this shadow is faced and dealt with the fame will only lead to increased isolation and loneliness. Being part of a community is working with others, not being admired and envied by them.

This is my point of departure. One I will take into my family and out into the larger community I inhabit. Many other men I meet through this work are moving into the next phase, and turning their heads to the future.

A child education psychologist recently told me he was working with an increasing number of children with learning disabilities. And over 80 percent were boys. This was not the usual "girls learn faster than boys" factor, but a growing number of children, overwhelmingly male, whose brains will apparently not learn the way that they have in the past. They come up against "blocks" which impede their learning abilities for a few years, although most recover by their teens.

Maybe we could listen to the symptom a little more, before we try and come up with the cure. Maybe we are being given a chance to review the education and socialization practices currently accepted as standard. It is possible that when a boy is put into a concentrated learning situation, centuries of male genetic coding are triggered. He moves automatically into competition, fighting for his place in the pecking order, and discards the emotions that hinder this linear progression. He steps onto the first rung of a long ladder that starts with the three Rs and ends up in the workplace. Maybe it is not early reading that will be important for future man, but more time to explore the world. To increase the experience of nature and nurture, before he is sat in front of a desk for what may prove to be the rest of his life. In *Raising a Son*, Don and Jeanne Elium write:

> Our culture expects parents to pressure boys into their male roles
> from the beginning. Boy babies are dressed in blue—not pink!—
> and are given balls to play with—not dolls! This early push into

male stereotypes erodes a boy's tender emotional side and his creative imagination, both vital to his ability to love. Boys need to unfold as children within a structure that will guide their male forces, not imprison them.

(p.149)

Maybe the boys we currently think of as disabled are struggling to break out of this cultural prison, and become more abled than their fathers, in ways we are not yet aware of.

Another man, who has run men's groups in young offenders institutions for several years, is developing a program called "Thunder Road," which will take small groups of these young men into carefully supervised residential settings over the course of a year. To let them talk, and listen to older men; to let them experience being in a non-punitive community of men; to allow their imagination to expand with the ritual techniques that men have used for thousands of years to help find a sense of purpose and a place in their world. Many of these young men got into trouble for deeds designed to attract the attention of others. Maybe their imagination can offer them more constructive ways of seeking attention in the future.

Dudley Young suggests that: "If the young are not given proper images to dream upon, they will dream the improper, and civilization will suffer" (*Origins of the Sacred*, p. xii). A male youth is looking for danger and the possibility of death, and any car insurance company has the statistics to prove it. This need was recognized and catered to for millennia, through the trials and metaphorical death of initiation. Now, in the vacuum of modern times, can this dangerous energy be conveniently disposed of simply because we may no longer need it to hunt animals or defend our borders? I don't think so.

We suffer a double bind. Not only do we lack the mentors and the ritual opportunities to undergo initiation, we lack the metaphorical imagination to recognize such an opportunity if it did occur. In a recent American study of literacy, a group of teenag-

221

ers and a group of pensioners were shown a music video and read a poem. The pensioners couldn't follow the video, but grasped the meaning of the poem; the teenagers understood the message of the video, but couldn't see any meaning in the poem. The leap into the imagination is being lost, ironed out by a visual literacy, an addiction to the small screen which may seem progressive now, but prove disastrous later on.

The Office for Public Management held a recent meeting to discuss the possibility and desirability of "Men's Development in Organization." Do men need to be educated, or re-educated to deal with the shifting gender balance in the workplace? To make decisions in a less patriarchal way? To set up men's groups to discuss problems? My personal paranoia says that self-development in an organization is a contradiction in terms. Another voice wants to ask for more flexibility in working hours and job sharing. To reduce the pressure on working men so that there is time to develop something, anything, outside the workplace. Or go on living with the ugly fact that by far the most popular (i.e. frequent) hour for a Western man to have a heart attack is around 9 a.m. on a Monday morning.

Old men too have lost their place of honor, and are more likely to be locked out of the way in a retirement home, rather than welcomed for their unique knowledge and eccentric wisdom. There are few sights more moving at men's conferences than when those men over sixty are asked to come and sit at the front. Applause inevitably turns into a standing ovation as us younger men marvel at the mere fact of the survival of these elders. Many of them shed tears of gratitude and pride, having never been recognized and honored in this way before. Most of them worry about a "useless" retirement, unable to look forward to the promise of freedom. And the suicide rate among older men is rising.

In October 1994 Wild Dance Events organized the first mythopoetic, multi-cultural men's event in England. I hope it will be the first of many, and that the interest and involvement achieved in America can be reflected over here. At the most recent weeklong multi-cultural conference over there the feared young gang members were indeed present. They came with attitude, anger, and resentment at all older men, who had done nothing for them, and left them with no hope for the future. By the end of the event one of these young men asked an older teacher if he would come and spend a weekend with him and the rest of his gang and tell them mythic stories. He wanted to try and turn the heads of the gang so they could see a sustainable future—and find a place in the ongoing cultural story. He wanted them to hear the stories of descent and survival that groups of men have drawn courage from for so many centuries. In a sense, maybe, he was wanting to turn his street gang into a men's group.

A good friend recently asked me to help him plan his son's thirteenth birthday celebration. He invited the family's closest friends for the occasion. After a drink and introductions the men left the women and took his son into a tent that had been set up in the garden. We stayed there for two hours. We took turns to talk to this budding man, telling tales of wounds, journeys, and experiences we had undergone at his age, and attempting to draw lessons from them. Then we each gave him a present to seal the gift of our story. At first the men were almost as terrified as the boy, so unusual was the task at hand, but gradually the sacred importance of what we were trying to do dispelled all fear. By the end, the warmth we felt in the giving had taught us as much as it had taught him. It felt like a step in the right direction. To finish we spoke an old African song:

> Do not seek too much fame,
> but do not seek obscurity.
> Be proud.
> But do not remind the world of your deeds.
> Excel when you must,
> but do not excel the world.
> Many heroes are not yet born,
> many have already died.
> To be alive to hear this song is a victory.

(*The Rag and Bone Shop of the Heart*, p. 498)

SELECTED BIBLIOGRAPHY

(including suggested further reading)

Jeremiah Abrams and Connie Zweig, *Meeting the Shadow* (Los Angeles, Jeremy P. Tarcher Inc., 1991)

Aleksandr Afanas'Ev (ed.), *Russian Fairy Tales* (New York, Pantheon Books, 1945)

Ean Begg, *Myth and Today's Consciousness* (London, Coventure Ltd., 1984)

Bruno Bettelheim, *The Uses of Enchantment - The Meaning and Importance of Fairy Tales* (London, Penguin Books, 1991)

William Blake, *The Complete Poems* (London, Penguin Books, 1977)

Robert Bly, *Iron John - A Book About Men* (Shaftesbury, Dorset, Element Books Ltd., 1991)

—*A Little Book on the Human Shadow* (New York, Harper and Row, 1988)

—*News of the Universe - Poems of Twofold Consciousness* (San Francisco, Sierra Club Books, 1980)

—*Robert Bly - Selected Poems* (New York, Harper and Row, 1986)

Robert Bly (ed. and tr.), *Selected Poems of Lorca and Jimenez* (Boston, Beacon Press, 1973)

—*Selected Poems of Rainer Maria Rilke* (New York, Harper and Row, 1981)

Robert Bly, James Hillman, Michael Meade (ed.), *The Rag and Bone Shop of the Heart - Poems for Men* (New York, HarperCollins, 1992)

Jean Shinoda Bolen, *Gods in Everyman - A New Psychology of Men's Lives and Loves* (New York, HarperCollins, 1989)

Jimmy Boyle, *A Sense of Freedom* (London, Pan Books, 1977)

John Bradshaw, *Healing the Shame That Binds You* (Deerfield Beach, FL, Health Communications Inc., 1988)

Joseph Campbell, *The Hero With a Thousand Faces* (London, Paladin, 1988)

—*Myths to Live By* (New York, Viking Penguin, 1972)

Louise Carus Mahdi (ed.), *Betwixt and Between, Patterns of Mascuhne and Feminine Initiation* (La Salle, IL, Open Court, 1987)

Tom Chetwynd, *A Dictionary of Symbols* (London, HarperCollins, 1982)

Alla B. Chinen, *Beyond the Hero - Classic Stories of Men in Search of Soul* (New York, Putnam, 1993)

Edward F. Edinger, *Ego and Archetype - Individuation and the Religious Function of the Psyche* (New York, Viking Penguin Inc., 1972)

Mircea Eliade, *Rites and Symbols of Initiation - The Mysteries of Birth and Rebirth* (Woodstock, CT, Spring Publications, 1995)

—*Shamanism - Archaic Techniques of Ecstasy* (Princeton, NJ, Princeton University Press, 1964)

Don and Jeanne Elium, *Raising A Son* (Oregon, Beyond Words Publishing, Inc., 1992)

Merle A. Fossum and Marilyn J. Mason, *Facing Shame - Families in Recovery* (New York, W. W. Norton and Company, 1986)

Selected Bibliography

Marie-Louise von Franz, *Shadow and Evil in Fairy Tales* (Boston, Shambala Publications, 1987)

J. G. Frazer, *The Golden Bough* (London, Macmillan Press, 1922)

Jacob and Wilhelm Grimm, *Selected Tales* (London, Penguin Books, 1982)

James Hillman, *Puer Papers* (Woodstock, CT, Spring Publications, 1979)

—*Loose Ends - Primary Papers in Archetypal Psychology* (Woodstock, CT, Spring Publications, 1975)

—*Notes on White Supremacy* (Woodstock, CT, Spring Journal, 1986)

—*Interviews* (Woodstock, CT, Spring Publications, 1983)

—*Facing the Gods* (Woodstock, CT, Spring Publications, 1980)

James Hillman and Michael Ventura, *We've Had a Hundred Years of Psychotherapy - And the World's Getting Worse* (San Francisco, Harper, 1992)

Liam Hudson and Bernadine Jacot, *The Way Men Think - Intellect, Intimacy and the Erotic Imagination* (London, Yale University Press, 1991)

Ivan Illich, *Gender* (Berkeley, Heyday Books, 1982)

Robert A. Johnson, *He - Understanding Masculine Psychology* (King of Prussia PA, Religious Publishing Company, 1974)

C. G. Jung, *Symbols of Transformation* (Princeton, NJ, Princeton University Press, 1956)

Gershen Kaufman, *Shame - The Power of Caring* (Rochester Vermont, Schenkman Books, Inc., 1980)

Sam Keen, *Fire in the Belly - On Being A Man* (New York, Bantam Books, 1991)

D. H. Lawrence, *Selected Poems* (London, Penguin, 1972)

Li-Young Lee, *City In Which I Love You* (New York, BOA Editions Ltd., 1990)

Wayne Liebman, *Tending the Fire - The Ritual Men's Group* (St. Paul, MN, Ally Press, 1991)

Haki Madhubuti, *Black Men: Obsolete, Single, Dangerous? - The Afrikan-American Family in Transition* (Chicago, Third World Press, 1990)

—*Killing Memory, Seeking Ancestors* (Detroit, Lotus Press, 1987)

—*Earthquakes and Sunrise Missions* (Chicago, Third World Press, 1986)

Gregory Max Vogt, *Return to Father - Archetypal Dimensions of the Patriarch* (Woodstock, CT, Spring Publications, 1991)

Michael Meade, *Men and the Water of Life - Initiation and the Tempering of Men* (New York, HarperCollins, 1993)

Alice Miller, *The Drama of Being A Child* (London, Faber and Faber Ltd., 1983)

—*For Your Own Good* (London, Faber and Faber Ltd., 1983)

—*Banished Knowledge - Facing Childhood Injuries* (London, Virago Press Ltd., 1990)

Robert Moore and Douglas Gillette, *King Warrior Magician Lover - Rediscovering the Archetypes of the Mature Masculine* (New York, HarperCollins, 1990)

Thomas Moore, *Care of the Soul - A Guide for Cultivating Depth and Sacredness in Everyday Life* (New York, HarperCollins, 1992)

—*Soul Mates - Honoring the Mysteries of Love and Relationship* (Dorset, Element Books Ltd., 1994)

Selected Bibliography

Clarissa Pinkola Estes, *Women Who Run with the Wolves - Myths and Stories of the Wild Woman Archetype* (New York, Ballantine Books, 1992)

Paul Radin (ed.), *African Folk Tales* (New York, Schocken Books, 1983)

Robin Skynner and John Cleese, *Families and How to Survive Them* (London, Methuen, 1983)

Malidoma Somé, *Ritual - Power, Healing and Community* (Portland, OR, Swan Raven and Company, 1993)

—*Of Water and the Spirit - Ritual Magic and Initiation in the Life of an African Shaman* (New York, Putnam, 1994)

William Stafford, *The Darkness Around Us Is Deep* (New York, HarperCollins, 1993)

Marcia Stark and Gynne Stern, *The Dark Goddess - Dancing with the Shadow* (Freedom, CA, The Crossing Press, 1993)

Deborah Tannen, *You Just Don't Understand - Women and Men in Conversation* (London, Virago Press Ltd., 1992)

Keith Thompson (ed.), *To Be A Man* (Los Angeles, Jeremy P. Tarcher, 1991)

Alvin Toffler, *The Eco-Spasm Report* (New York, Bantam Books, 1975)

Victor Turner, *The Ritual Process - Structure and Anti-Structure* (New York, Cornell University Press, 1969)

Arnold Van Gennep, *The Rites of Passage* (Chicago, University of Chicago Press, 1960)

Michael Ventura, *Letters at 3 am - Reports on Endarkenment* (Woodstock, CT, Spring Publications, 1993)

Claude Whitmyer (ed.), *In the Company of Others - Making Community in the Modern World* (Los Angeles, Jeremy P. Tarcher, 1983)

W. B. Yeats, *Yeat's Poems* (London, Macmillan, 1989)

Dudley Young, *Origins of the Sacred - The Ecstasies of Love and War* (London, Little, Brown and Company, 1991)

RESOURCES

Wild Dance Events

Produces conferences and workshops in England with Robert Bly, James Hiliman, Michael Meade, Malidoma Somé, and others—for men and women—in ritual, mythology, gender, and multi-cultural issues. For information and news of upcoming events contact: Wild Dance Events, P.O. Box 6165, London SW6 6XB, England. Tel: 0171-813 4260.

Limbus

Produces workshops with Michael Meade, Malidoma Somé, and others throughout the United States. Also book and tape store containing many recommended books and tapes. Write or call: Limbus, P.O. Box 364, Vashon, WA 98070. Tel: (206) 463-9387.

Mosaic

A multi-cultural foundation which produces and raises funds to bring together men from different racial and ethnic backgrounds. Address same as Limbus above.

Ally Press

Publishes a magazine/newsletter called *Dragonsmoke* which includes Robert Bly's American lecture/workshop schedule. Book and tape store for many recommended books and tapes, especially poetry. Write to: Ally Press, 524 Orleans St., St. Paul, MN 55107.

London Convivium for Archetypal Studies

Organizes conferences and special events related to the ideas of James Hillman and archetypal psychology. Publishes an annual magazine of essays and poetry called *Sphinx*. For further details write to: London Convivium for Archetypal Studies, P.O. Box 417, London NW3 7RJ, England.

RECOMMENDED AUDIO CASSETTES

Robert Bly: *Fairy Tales for Men and Women; Iron John and the Male Mode of Feeling; Men and the Wound; The Naive Male; The Power of Shame; What Stories Do We Need?*

Robert Bly, James Hillman, Michael Meade: *Men and the Life of Desire.*

Robert Bly, John Lee, Robert Moore, Malidoma Somé: *Who Welcomes the Newborn to this World.*

Robert Bly, Michael Meade: *The Inner King and Queen.*

Robert Bly, Deborah Tannen: *Men and Women Talking Together.*

Robert Bly, Marion Woodman: *Facing the Shadow in Men and Women; The Divine Child.*

Clarissa Pinkola Estes: *The Creative Fire; Warming the Stone Child; The Boy Who Married an Eagle; How to Love a Woman.*

James Hillman: *A Blue Fire, Part I; A Blue Fire, Part II.*

Michael Meade: *The Mythology of Gender; Thresholds of Change; Warriors on the Healing Path.*

James Hillman, Michael Meade, Malidoma Somé: *Images of Initiation.*

Michael Meade, Robert Moore: *The Great Self Within.*

Robert Moore: *Healing the Masculine; Masculine Potentials; The Four Couples Within; The Trickster Archetype.*

Thomas Moore: *On Creativity; Care of the Soul; Soul Mates.*

Malidoma Somé: *Nature, Magic and Community.*

Some of the above can be found in large bookshops, or psychology/New Age bookshops. Nearly all of them can be ordered through Limbus (see Resources).

Spring Publications

FURTHER READING

HEALING FICTION • JAMES HILLMAN

Hillman's main deconstruction of therapy asks "What does the soul want?" and answers "Fictions that heal." Examining the three great originators of depth psychology: Freud, Jung and Adlerù these chapters look again at what is really meant by "case history," "active imagination" and "inferiority feelings." Especially in examples of case materials of active imagination, we learn that the soul heals by telling itself a better story, an "as if" fiction that dissolves the belief system that keeps the soul locked in misery.

145 pp. ISBN 0-88214-363-8 Psychology/Recovery

OEDIPUS VARIATIONS • KARL KERÉNYI AND JAMES HILLMAN

Kerényi elucidates both the ancient Oedipus myth, red-haired temper, swollen feet and crossroads, and dramatic versions from Seneca to Eliot. Hillman inverts the emphasis of Father Freud's famous complex: why do fathers kill their sons? He shows that, in addition to the curse, murder, incest and disease, the myth contains beauty, blessing, love and loyalty. (Available from Spring Audio: Hillman's The Death of Oedipus tape.)

170 pp. ISBN 0-88214-219-4 Mythology/Psychology

RETURN TO FATHER • GREGORY MAX VOGT

Can the impoverished male soul and body be restored? This manifesto gives historical and archetypal substance to the new patriarch and challenges each man to revive in a new way the tradition of hunter and builder, lover and philosopher, protector of society and visionary. Includes bibliography. "This is one of those books that can make you feel good about being a man." Seattle M.E.N.

169 pp. ISBN 0-88214-347-6 Psychology/Men's Studies

RITES AND SYMBOLS OF INITIATION • MIRCEA ELIADE

Organizing data from cultures the world over, Eliade lays out the basic patterns of initiationùgroup puberty rites, entrance into secret cults, individual shamanic instruction and visions, heroic rites of passage, women's mysteries and affirms the tie between humans and the cosmos. Michael Meade's new foreword addresses the value of Eliade's work at the end of the millennium, when we must cross over a critical threshold.

175 pp. ISBN 0-88214-358-1 Religion/Men's Studies/Anthropology

For a free catalog write:

Spring Publications, Inc.
299 East Quassett Road, Woodstock, CT 06281
tel: (860) 974-3428 fax: (860) 974-3195

or look up our on-line catalog at HTTP://WWW.NECA.COM/~SPRING